AUDLEY END

D1484858

CONTENTS

Published by English Heritage
Copyright © English Heritage 1997
First published 1997. Reprinted 1998, 1999. Revised edition 2002. Reprinted 2004. Revised reprint 2005. Reprinted 2007

Edited by Kate Jeffrey
Designed by Carroll Associates
Printed in England by the colourhouse C80 07/07
ISBN 1 85074 821 7

Unless otherwise stated, all the photographs were taken by the English Heritage Photographic Unit and remain the copyright of English Heritage. Every effort has been made to trace the copyright holders of the illustrations and we apologise in advance for any unintentional omission, which we would be pleased to correct in any subsequent edition of this book.

Acknowledgements
English Heritage would like to thank Lord Braybrooke for the generous loan of many of the paintings, the silver collection and other items, and also for his kind permission to reproduce photographs of many of the items. We would also like to thank Mr (formerly Corporal) Peter Howe for sharing his wartime reminiscences of Audley End. The Tryon Palace Historic Sites and Gardens, an agency of the North Carolina Department of Cultural Resources, kindly allowed us to examine and copy for the Dining Parlour the rare turkey-pattern Axminster carpet in its collections. In preparing this guidebook the authors have drawn extensively on the earlier English Heritage handbook written by Paul Drury and Ian Gow.

Note to visitors
English Heritage is committed to preserving Audley End for future generations to enjoy, and asks for your help in achieving this. Please respect the rules about not smoking or eating in the house, and refrain from touching any of the items on display.

INTRODUCTION

Richard Neville, third Lord Braybrooke (1783-1858) by John Hoppner

Audley End is one of the great sights of East Anglia: a spectacular Jacobean mansion set in an outstanding landscaped park. Now only a third of its original size, its history is one of vastly fluctuating fortunes, with episodes of ambitious development followed by periods of decline and retrenchment. This story is evident throughout the house and park: in the changing use of the rooms, the contrasting tastes in interiors and garden styles, and the diverse collections of paintings and objects, all of which reflect the owners and their times.

Originally one of the great Jacobean 'prodigy' houses, surrounded by vast formal gardens, Audley End was built in 1603-14 by the first Earl of Suffolk with the express intention of providing accommodation for visiting royalty. Within four years of its completion, however, Suffolk had fallen from favour, and over the following centuries the house was gradually reduced and altered. In the second half of the eighteenth century Audley End was given a new lease of life by Sir John Griffin Griffin, who created an elegant suite of reception rooms with the help of the celebrated architect Robert Adam, and a superb landscaped park largely designed by 'Capability' Brown. Further enhancements were made on Sir John's elevation to the peerage as Lord Howard de Walden in 1784.

Above all the interiors that can be seen today represent the taste of the third Lord Braybrooke, who created a splendid sequence of first-floor reception rooms in the 1820s. The romantic 'Jacobean' character of these opulent rooms, and of the elaborate flower garden or parterre below, is a tribute to the third lord's antiquarian interest in the early history of his house.

Sir John Griffin Griffin formed the basis of an ancestral picture collection, comprising family portraits and 'Old Master' paintings. In the nineteenth century the painting, furniture and silver collections were further enlarged by the Neville family through a gradual process of inheritance and marriage.

During the Second World War Audley End served as the secret headquarters of the Polish section of the Special Operations Executive. The house was purchased for the nation in 1948 and is now in the care of English Heritage.

Visitors begin in the formal open space of the Great Hall, then mount the stairs, as their nineteenth-century predecessors would have done, to the sequence of grand reception rooms created by the third Lord Braybrooke in the 1820s. After passing through a series of family and guest rooms they descend to the ground floor to see part of the nineteenth-century service area, followed by a fine suite of neoclassical reception rooms created by Robert Adam in the late eighteenth century.

The fact that Audley End has two sets of reception rooms requires explanation. Historically, they did not coexist: the original Robert Adam suite was partially destroyed by the third Lord Braybrooke when he introduced his new reception rooms upstairs. This arrangement was reversed in the 1960s by the Ministry of Works, which recreated the Adam rooms, thereby destroying work by the third lord. Today's conservators would be more likely to present the house as it has evolved over time, giving an insight into changing tastes and patterns of use.

The programme of research, conservation and restoration is continuous. RIGHT *Hand-weaving a silk tissue for the festoon curtains in the Great Drawing Room.* BELOW *Restoration of the parterre garden was preceded by a pioneering project in garden archaeology*

The interiors are dimly lit for conservation reasons, though the house would have appeared in a similar light throughout the period of family occupancy since electricity was not installed until the Second World War. Pictures are hung in their historic locations, often densely arranged. Unobtrusive barriers and coverings have been installed to protect the historic carpets and furniture, and visitors are requested kindly not to touch fragile items.

At the dawn of the twenty-first century Audley End is far from a static museum piece. Under English Heritage, exciting plans for its future development are under way. We are currently focusing on opening up service areas, such as the kitchen, dairy and laundry, which have never before been properly displayed to the public. The year 2000 saw the opening of the newly restored kitchen garden, in association with the Henry Doubleday Research Association. In addition, Audley End is brought to life every year by a stimulating programme of special events, culminating in a series of spectacular open-air summer concerts (telephone 01793 414910 for an Events Diary or 020 8233 7435 for concert information).

This guidebook begins with a descriptive tour of the house for use during your visit. It is followed by a history of the house, gardens and collections which you may wish to read at home after your visit.

A TOUR OF AUDLEY END HOUSE

Please refer to the two floor plans on the front flap for the location of the rooms described in the tour.

1 ENTRANCE HALL

Visitors pass through the Jacobean porch, with its exuberant decoration, and into the house by way of the great oak door surmounted by an allegorical carving depicting the rewards of Peace.

Although the Entrance Hall is small and somewhat austere, it has served as one of the main entrances to Audley End since its construction in the early seventeenth century. This was originally the screens passage, which defined the separation between the service areas to the left, and the symbolic heart of the household, the Great Hall, to the right. The fact that entry was through the screens passage reflects the survival of the medieval arrangement of houses into the early seventeenth century; by contrast, the exterior facade reflected a new sense of classical order, with two porches arranged symmetrically on either side of the bay window of the Great Hall. In the nineteenth century the Entrance Hall was brought increasingly into the 'family' side of the house with the introduction of furniture and paintings, although a reminder of the traditional emphasis on the 'service' side was retained in the form of the set of leather fire buckets hanging from the oak beams. The furniture includes a marble-topped table moved here from the Great Hall sometime after 1836, a musical long-case clock, an oak armchair and cane-seated walnut chairs of the late seventeenth century. This eclectic combination of furnishings from many different periods is typical of the antiquarian taste of the third Lord Braybrooke.

2 GREAT HALL

The Great Hall dates from the building of the house (1603-14). In the Middle Ages households were run according to a complex system of hierarchy and deference, at the heart of which was the Great Hall, where communal meals took place. By the seventeenth century this system had largely disappeared and the hall form survived essentially as an anachronistic status symbol. The head of a household now generally preferred to withdraw to more private areas for eating and entertaining, although servants may have continued to take meals here.

The Great Hall rises through two storeys and is lit by five large windows on the west front, the centre window projecting in a large bow. The main architectural focus is the Jacobean oak screen at the north end, carved in high relief with grotesque masks and characteristic pairs of herms (male and female half-figures), raised on richly ornamented pedestals. The upper part of the screen forms the front of the gallery and is embellished with scrolling strapwork. The roof is largely original, although renewed and repaired. Each of the plaster panels is separated by oak beams and contains coloured crests of the Howard family.

The interior of the Great Hall as it appears today was largely created by the third Lord Braybrooke in the 1820s. The screened Hall, with its display of heraldry, was a perfect expression of his antiquarian scholarship and nostalgia for the past. An occasion for medieval-style hospitality offered itself in 1852, when the Great Hall was used for a dinner celebrating the marriage of the third lord's eldest son; such a setting served to emphasise the antiquity of the family's lineage.

To recreate the Hall's original ambience, the third lord first had to undo the work of his eighteenth-century predecessors, removing white paint from the roof timbers and screen. The old and decayed wall panelling was replaced in 1829. The chimneypiece was enlarged and remodelled with old fragments, including the carved arms of Charles, seventh Earl of Suffolk and his wife, Arabella. Silk banners bearing the arms of owners of the manor of Walden from the twelfth to the nineteenth centuries were hung from the wall brackets on regimental lances. By contrast, modern innovations aimed at creating contemporary standards of comfort included the replacement of the old

ABOVE *Detail of the north porch door. This was probably intended as the queen's entrance to the house; the carving depicts the rewards of peace*

BELOW *Marble pedestal in the antique taste, purchased from Robert Adam in 1773 for the display of sculpture in the Great Hall*

OPPOSITE *The Great Hall as it was decorated and furnished by the third Lord Braybrooke in the 1820s. At the far end is the early seventeenth-century oak screen*

casement windows with sash windows containing large glass plates in 1829.

The third lord used his inherited collections to create an idiosyncratic interior featuring objects esteemed for their age and historical associations. Two Coade stone figures, originally made for Sir John Griffin Griffin's neoclassical library, were painted to resemble oak and fitted into the chimneypiece, while the marble pedestal, purchased in 1773 from Robert Adam, was retained in the window bay. Reflecting the third lord's interest in British and medieval antiquities were a selection of oak carvings and furniture, notably the walnut chairs and the oak and inlaid court cupboard. The Flemish carving in the seventeenth-century-style case was purchased at an auction of Dutch furniture in 1826.

The Hall was further embellished with Indian shields, various fine firearms and a collection of swords. The helmet and epaulettes of two of the third lord's sons, who were killed during the Crimean War (1854-6), hang to the left of the chimneypiece.

The full-length portraits above the panelling are Cornwallis family pictures, while those on either side of the stone screen are mostly family members, monarchs and allies. The most notable portrait, hanging above the heating vent on the east wall, is of Margaret Audley, Duchess of Norfolk, by Hans Eworth; her son, the first Earl of Suffolk, was the builder of the great Jacobean house.

3 STAIRCASE

The stone screen at the south end of the Hall has historically been associated with the architect Sir John Vanbrugh, who carried out other work at Audley End in about 1708, although it may be the work of another architect, Nicholas Dubois. Dubois designed the staircase, which provides a ceremonial approach up to the Saloon, during the mid-1720s. The Jacobean chapel was being demolished at this time and it seems that fragments were incorporated into the columns and entablature (lintel) framing the doorcase at the top of the stairs. The ceiling above the staircase is original, surviving from the Jacobean period. Nineteenth-century commentators considered these later features out of keeping with the rest of the Hall; Lord Braybrooke attributed it to the 'bad taste of Sir John Vanbrugh'.

4 SALOON

The Saloon is one of the most splendid of Audley End's interiors, the extravagance of the plaster ceiling befitting its Jacobean usage as the Great Chamber. Sir John Griffin Griffin retained this ceiling, with its thirty-two compartments, set between large pendants and outlined with patterned strapwork. According to Lord Braybrooke it was 'originally called the Fish Room, after the dolphins and sea-monsters represented in bold relief'. The frieze of Gothic quatrefoils probably dates from 1765-73, when Sir John first fitted out the Saloon. New panelling was installed with an elaborate frieze, and carved details were added from the demolished Long Gallery. The recesses within the round-headed arches were fitted with a series of ancestral portraits illustrating Sir John's descent from Sir Thomas Audley, the original recipient of Walden Abbey. The portraits of Sir John and his mother, and the early portraits of his Howard and Audley ancestors, were painted by the Italian artist Biagio Rebecca.

In 1784 Sir John was elevated to the peerage as Lord Howard de Walden, and over the following two years further decorative work was carried out to make the interior more splendid. As an acknowledgement of the family's ancient debt to the monarchy, Biagio Rebecca provided two more portraits – one of Henry VIII, who granted the abbey and its lands to Thomas Audley, and another of Elizabeth I, who created the barony of Howard de Walden. Rebecca also decorated the arms of the first Earl of Suffolk and his wife over the chimneypiece. At the same time the Saloon was painted white and enriched with gilding in the fashionable taste of the decade.

In place of Sir John's coordinated grandeur, Lord and Lady Braybrooke created an interior of their own time in the 1820s, transforming the

ABOVE *Dedication dated 1786, expressing Sir John's gratitude to those to whom he owed his position and ownership of Audley End*

TOP LEFT *Table top inlaid with pewter, brass and red tortoiseshell. Known as Boulle-work, this is a fine and early example of its type, mounted on an English oak base of the 1820s*

CENTRE *This mahogany sofa, made in about 1740, was reupholstered and painted in white and gilt to match the room. It was part of a suite of two sofas, eleven chairs and one stool*

OPPOSITE *The Saloon, with its seventeenth-century plaster ceiling, eighteenth-century family portraits and nineteenth-century carpet and furnishings*

ABOVE *The white ground carpet was made by Thomas Whitty of Axminster and was originally in the Saloon*

BELOW *A bust of the first Marquess Cornwallis by John Bacon RA. Above hangs a portrait of his grand-daughter, wife of the third Lord Braybrooke*

OPPOSITE *The Drawing Room, as furnished by the third Lord Braybrooke for his private use*

Saloon into a comfortable and informal living room. Visiting Audley End in 1847 Mrs Bancroft, wife of the American minister to England, described the Saloon thus: 'Not withstanding its vast size, the sofas and tables were so disposed all over the apartment as to give it the most friendly, warm and social aspect.'

The majority of Sir John's furniture remained in situ, placed against the walls in formal eighteenth-century style. By the 1850s, however, it was covered with loose covers of chintz, in colours chosen to complement the room's decorative scheme. Many contemporary pieces, such as the comfortable sofas, were simply loose-covered over the upholsterer's outer linen layer. This helped to create the informal air considered desirable in the early nineteenth century while also preserving furniture with fitted upholstery. The chairs flanking the chimneypiece were reupholstered in the nineteenth century; the needlework covers with a red quatrefoil ground surrounding conventional floral panels were probably made by the ladies of the family.

Furniture and soft furnishings introduced in the 1820s include the remarkable Axminster carpet, the circular Regency-period centre tables, around which groups of chairs could be informally placed, the rectangular rosewood sofa table (a new type), and some examples of fashionable French furniture. The pair of vitrines, or display cases, at the south end of the room are in the French style – although English-made – and contain family mementoes. Other furnishings were added to the Saloon as the century progressed, including the ottoman, a rare survival probably dating from the 1860s or 1870s.

The arrangement of plants on a table in the bay is illustrated in a watercolour of about 1850; plants were cultivated in greenhouses for interior display from the late eighteenth century. The curtains are reproductions of the light-damaged originals, which were of hand-woven damask and featured an eighteenth-century French pattern redrawn by a Spitalfields weaver. The colour red was Lord and Lady Braybrooke's first choice for their new reception rooms since it was particularly associated with ancient and noble interiors.

5 DRAWING ROOM

Lord Braybrooke created this room from two rooms belonging to the eighteenth-century State Bedroom suite. Paradoxically he fashioned an interior that was redolent of the seventeenth century, retained the white and gold decoration of the late eighteenth century, but was entirely of the 1820s in its function and furnishing. The ceiling was copied from the remains of the Jacobean

RIGHT *The South Library painted in about 1850. Its appearance has not altered since the early nineteenth century and, of all the rooms, it best expresses the continuity from one generation to another*

BELOW *Portrait of Lady Braybrooke, by Henry Pickersgill, 1834. Her husband hung it in his private Drawing Room*

CENTRE *Nineteenth-century visitors would have considered this walnut armchair, once the property of the poet Alexander Pope, one of the most evocative items at Audley End*

example in the adjoining South Library, while the frieze imitates details from the exterior porches. The Jacobean chimneypiece is possibly from the north wing of the house, brought here by Lord Braybrooke and fitted with an eighteenth-century steel grate from the State Dressing Room.

Lord Braybrooke used this room as his personal sitting room and hung it with the cream of Sir John's 'cabinet' pictures: Dutch, Italian and Flemish paintings of the type favoured by English gentlemen in the late eighteenth and early nineteenth centuries. The walls were hung with red flock wallpaper of an eighteenth-century design (since replaced), the traditional background for pictures. The third lord took obvious pride in this collection, formed by Sir John. Particularly fine are *On the Shore at Egmond aan Zee* (1642) and *View of the Valkhof at Nijmegen* (1646), which hang to the right and left of the chimneypiece. They are by Jan van Goyen, the seventeenth-century Dutch master of landscape. *The View of the Campanile and the Doge's Palace* by Canaletto was at Audley End by 1797, and two other Venetian views attributed to Canaletto's studio were acquired by the second Lord Braybrooke. The portrait of Lady Braybrooke, by H W Pickersgill was the only modern addition to the collection in this room.

The room was furnished with inherited pieces, such as the five chairs brought from the Saloon. The two firescreens, in the Chinese taste, were decorated by Louisa, Marchioness Cornwallis, Lady Braybrooke's mother, in a European technique imitating oriental lacquer known as 'japanning'. The modern English Boulle-style cabinets for the display of porcelain represent more orthodox tastes, as do the fine 'antique' examples of French furniture: the Louis XV-period clock on a

bracket and the two French writing tables. One is signed by the cabinet maker Montigny and is in the neoclassical style of the Louis XVI period, while the other is of an earlier date and in the rococo style, with floral marquetry, curved cabriole legs and scrolled ormolu (gilt bronze) mounts.

6 SOUTH LIBRARY

When the new Library was created in the 1820s, this room was turned into a private library and working area for Lord Braybrooke, where he gathered together his most prized relics. It contains the remnants of an original Jacobean ceiling and frieze and a neoclassical chimneypiece by Robert Adam, installed in the 1780s.

The white and gold bookcases have adjustable shelves to accommodate outsize volumes, particularly topographical works. The collection is typical of the period, while also reflecting the particular interests of the third and fourth lords. There are books on gardening and agriculture, a selection of family bibles, and eighteenth- and nineteenth-century travel books on Europe, Australia, New Zealand and the Pacific. As might be expected, there are a number of books on heraldry and genealogy as well as military history, and a good collection of monographs on other country houses and their collections. Books purchased by Sir John are distinguished by their red leather covering and a gold chequer pattern on the spine.

The four chairs installed here by Lord Braybrooke were originally part of Sir John's suite of furniture for the Saloon. A 1786 invoice describes their yellow-and-white ground upholstery as 'patent tapestry', supplied by Thomas Moore of Moorfields. The backs of all the chairs and the two sofas were mounted with Howard lion crests and coronets. The unusual table screen, with a gilt frame and silk embroidered panel, was originally made for the Lady's State Dressing Room. These eighteenth-century items contrast strongly with others in the room, but it is apparent that each item has been selected for its historical associations.

An item of particular interest to the third Lord Braybrooke and his contemporaries would have been the walnut armchair with a triangular seat. A brass plaque on the back seat rail records: 'This

chair once the property of Alexander Pope, was given as a keepsake to the nurse who attended him in his last illness. From her descendants it was obtained by Reverend Thomas Ashley, when Curate of the Parish of Binfield, and kindly presented by him to Lord Braybrooke in 1844.'

The library table is typical of early nineteenth-century furniture in seventeenth-century style. The 'metamorphic' armchair, with its distinctive Regency sabre legs, folds open to form library steps. The silk curtains are modern reproductions of one of Lord Braybrooke's most precious family relics. The originals were made of a crimson silk damask woven with the Neville saltire (a heraldic device similar to the St Andrew's cross), which had been presented in 1670 to his ancestor, Henry Nevill of Warfield, by Cosmo de Medici, the Grand Duke of Tuscany. Unlike other curtains in the house made during the nineteenth century, they were lined with silk as opposed to wool tammy, a mark of their importance.

The portraits of Sir John Griffin Griffin and his two wives, painted by Sir Benjamin West in 1772,

were originally hung in Sir John's Library on the ground floor. Sir John is wearing the star of the Order of the Bath which he received in 1761.

7 LIBRARY

The Library was a new interior created by the third Lord Braybrooke in an historical manner achieved through the careful copying of existing details in the house. The plaster ceiling was copied from a Jacobean ceiling in the Dining Room while the frieze imitates that of the South Library. The arrangement of bays flanked by pilasters reproduces that of Sir John's Saloon, with the addition of fixed shelving for books. The frieze with strapwork and grotesque masks, and the white and gold decoration, executed in 1829, also emulate the Saloon scheme. The chimneypiece was moved here from the Howard Bedroom in the north wing.

Throughout the eighteenth century libraries tended to be masculine preserves and somewhat austere in their furnishing. By the 1820s, however, it had become fashionable for all the family to use

ABOVE *The Library. The arms of the Audley and Neville families on the chimneypiece link to third lord's family with the early owners of the house*

ABOVE *George II by Robert Edge Pine. Lord Howard purchased the portrait from the artist in 1784, nearly twenty-five years after it was painted. It now hangs in the Dining Room*

OPPOSITE *The Dining Room. The table is set as it would have been for the dessert course in the 1870s and 1880s, using a mid-nineteenth-century dessert service*

the library as an informal sitting room, and the furnishings reflected this dual use. A comfortable environment was created by loose-covered sofas, which were intended to be placed at right-angles to the fire, and armchairs and other contemporary furniture types, such as the table for reading and writing in front of the sofa. The circular centre table, of fashionable amboyna wood, provided a focus for informal gatherings, while the oak portfolio stand could be opened up to examine large and precious volumes. The ebonised table with a green baize top was made for Lord Braybrooke, originally to contain the 'Scrapbook', a volume of accumulated prints, drawings and plans relating to the house. The American visitor Mrs Bancroft describes how social activities of a more relaxed nature took place in the Library. After breakfast and a tour of the house, 'We returned to the Library, a room as splendid as the Saloon, only instead of pictured panels it was surrounded by books in beautiful gilt bindings. In the immense bay window was a large Louis Quatorze table, round which the ladies all placed themselves at their embroidery, though I preferred looking over curious illuminated missals....' The Library accommodates many works of classical literature as well as volumes of standard eighteenth-century French and Italian literature, topographical and historical works on the English counties, archaeology and illustrated manuscripts.

The large bay window provided a good view over the parterre garden which was laid out in 1832. Although the morning light would have been favourable for needlework, reading or writing, it was also potentially damaging to the fragile fabric of the books. Several measures were taken to solve this problem, including inserting sash shutters into the window sill and fitting red striped blinds to the windows. The crimson damask curtains, trimmed with silk gimp (a looped braid) and held back with silk and wool tie-backs, are reproductions of originals which were in place by 1836.

The 'Brussels' carpet (as loop-piles were called from the time they were first made in the eighteenth century) is a reproduction also, seamed and laid in exactly the same way as the worn and faded original. It has vivid contemporary colours but draws on the Gothic motif of interlaced quatrefoils for its design.

8 DINING ROOM

The Dining Room was originally two Jacobean rooms, the plaster ceilings and friezes of which were retained when the dividing wall was removed. A Jacobean chimneypiece was copied to provide unity between the two rooms. As was customary in dining rooms, Lord Braybrooke hung the walls with

portraits: a combination of Neville (brought from the family seat, Billingbear), Cornwallis and Howard relatives. Apart from a single loss in this room, this remarkable collection, formed by inheritance and marriage, has been kept together to this day.

Above the sideboard at the far end of the room is a portrait of Lady Braybrooke's grandfather, the first Marquess Cornwallis, in his Garter robes. To its left is a portrait of her mother Louisa, Marchioness Cornwallis, by Sir Thomas Lawrence.

The richness of the interior fittings is augmented by the large hand-knotted Axminster carpet and wool velvet plush curtains with a pelmet trimmed with bullion fringe. The silk and wool tie-backs, which are modern reproductions, indicate the original colourings of this curtain scheme.

By contrast, the furniture was more functional and contemporary. One of the mahogany sideboards and the sectioned dining table are in the style of about 1810 and probably date from the second Lord Braybrooke's time. The second sideboard was probably made later for reasons of symmetry. The table could be sized according to the number of diners and the unused sections on their individual pedestals could then be used as side-tables. The simple mahogany chairs were originally covered with green leather, a material traditionally used in dining rooms as it was hard-wearing and did not retain the smell of food.

The Audley End accounts include details of 'Persons Dining' in the years 1867-75, in the time of Charles, fifth Lord Braybrooke. The figures for July 1872 show that on 14 July only three visitors dined, but that on 16 July ninety-five visitors were entertained. The average monthly figure was 700-900, of which the bulk was made up of servants. The accompanying remarks give some indication of the variety of visitors, such as 'Music Master', 'Miss Mildmay & Maid' and '14 for Dinner & one Gentleman for Lunch'.

9 SOUTH LOBBY

This area was a passage for guests and family moving from the Saloon to the Dining Room. It would also have formed the point of entry for the food, a highly unsatisfactory arrangement according to accepted nineteenth-century protocol, which dictated that service activities should be kept out of sight.

The oak staircase is the finer of two surviving staircases from the Jacobean house. It was embellished with further decoration by the third lord. The stairs lead up to bedrooms, probably for guests, and up another small staircase to a set of servants' rooms at the front of the house.

The landing area is hung with a set of five

RIGHT *The entrance of the Picture Gallery from the North Lobby in about 1850, much as it is today*

seventeenth-century portraits of Ralph Grey, second Lord Grey of Werke, his wife, two sons and daughter Catherine, who married Richard Neville of Billingbear. The portraits accompanied Catherine to Billingbear, and the third lord brought them to Audley End. They are by the court artist Sir Peter Lely and have matching contemporary frames, exquisitely carved with undercutting and scrolling on the corners. The miniatures are largely Griffin portraits and formed part of the Countess of Portsmouth's inheritance. The finest example is by Nicholas Hilliard of Sir Thomas Griffin of Dingley, dated 1599.

10 PICTURE GALLERY

This gallery was formed by Sir John Griffin Griffin after 1763 to connect the north and south wings at first-floor level. The plaster ceiling was created in Jacobean style with interlacing strapwork. Sir John furnished it with country-style armchairs and hung it with a motley display of prints, watercolours and maps.

The third Lord Braybrooke chose to develop the room's potential as a picture gallery by introducing a series of important sixteenth-, seventeenth- and eighteenth-century Cornwallis portraits originating from Lady Braybrooke's ancestral homes, Brome Hall and Culford in Suffolk. The earliest portraits date from the sixteenth century, notably a portrait attributed to George Gower of Sir Thomas Cornwallis, the builder of Brome Hall, in 1558. Other fine portraits include that of Charles, second Lord Cornwallis by John Michael Wright dating from the 1660s, and the Hon Henrietta Maria Cornwallis by Sir Peter Lely. At the far end of the Picture Gallery, above the display cabinet, is a painting of Billingbear, the Neville family seat in Berkshire.

BELOW *The Picture Gallery photographed in 1891, with its fitted cases of natural history specimens and two extraordinary swan firescreens (which have not survived)*

Throughout the nineteenth century the Picture Gallery served as another comfortable and informal family sitting room, connecting the family bedrooms with the reception rooms. The fourth lord's natural history collection gradually accumulated here, initially displayed in cases of various sizes piled up in an arbitrary fashion, but mounted in fitted oak cases soon after the fourth lord's succession in 1858. (See page 54 for a discussion of the natural history collection). By 1891 a miscellaneous collection of ceramics embellished the tops of the cases, including oriental ceramics, ancient Delft ware and Sir John's blue and white Worcester jugs and washbowls, originally used in the State Apartment.

The red wool plush curtains and pelmets trimmed with bullion fringe date from the early twentieth century; at the same time the floor was relaid with a Brussels carpet in two shades of red and black, with a seaweed-pattern ground and entwined floral border.

11 NORTH LOBBY

From this level the staircase leads up to family bedrooms and to the nineteenth-century nurseries used by the third Lord Braybrooke's children.

The case to the left of the door from the Picture Gallery contains a pair of Great Bustards, once common on Salisbury Plain but now long extinct. Two family portraits, in pierced rococo-style frames, hang above this case and that on the other side. The gilded plaster cast of the Corbridge Lanx, hanging to the left of the marble-topped heating vent, illustrates the fourth lord's interest in archaeology. This celebrated late Roman dish was discovered at Corbridge in Northumberland in 1735.

12 CHAPEL VESTIBULE

In the Jacobean period this area was the music gallery overlooking the Great Hall. Subsequently it served as the family entrance to the Chapel. The pictures have religious themes and represent

NATIONAL MONUMENTS RECORD

conventional nineteenth-century piety. Mrs Bancroft relates how in 1847 the guests would assemble in the Picture Gallery at half-past nine before entering the Chapel for morning prayers.

13 CHAPEL

Sir John Griffin Griffin's chapel is a rare surviving example of a chapel in the late eighteenth-century Gothick style, with all its furniture intact. By the 1820s private chapels were becoming less common and, if the third lord had pursued his initial intention of converting the Chapel into a dining room, it may not have been replaced elsewhere. The third lord disliked its profusely ornamented fan vaulting, arcading and columns made of timber, lath and plaster painted to imitate stone. He objected to this essentially decorative interpretation of the Gothic style, which he considered archaeo-logically dishonest.

In the late 1760s Sir John commissioned the master builder John Hobcroft to produce the designs and carry out the work for his new chapel,

including all the furnishings. The floor was covered with an oilcloth painted to simulate a Portland and Bremen stone pavement; the current covering is a reproduction. The Chapel was further embellished in 1786 with heraldic decoration linking the Audley, Griffin and Howard families.

Morning prayers were said in the Chapel every day except on Sundays when the family joined the local community in Saffron Walden Church. The family pew was comfortably furnished with a set of painted chairs inset with the Griffin crest. Although re-covered in recent years, the hassocks are also original. Other comforts were provided by a Wilton carpet and a fire burning in the chimneypiece. The indoor servants sat in the organ gallery while the outdoor servants and kitchen staff, who entered via a staircase from the service areas below, used the plain oak benches and brown leather kneelers. These functional items, together with the communion table, were made by the estate joiners.

The carved chair and lectern are made of olive wood and were carved by the accomplished

ABOVE *The interior of the Chapel. The stained and painted glass windows of 'Our Saviour's Last Supper' was made by William Peckitt of York in 1771*

furniture-maker and carver Sefferin Alkin. The plaster half-size model of the first Marquess Cornwallis was made by Charles Rossi from the Marquess's tomb monument in St Paul's Cathedral. It was given to the third lord in 1835 by the Marquess's daughter, Lady Mary Singleton.

14 LADY BRAYBROOKE'S SITTING ROOM

This and the following rooms form a private apartment used in the nineteenth century by the third Lord Braybrooke and his wife. The wallpaper is a modern reproduction of a design used throughout the apartment dating from about 1830.

The third Lady Braybrooke used this as a dressing room and morning room. It was an informal environment in which she could conduct everyday activities such as letter-writing. Comfortable armchairs were covered with chintz loose covers to match the wallpaper and curtains. Other furniture included the French corner cupboards of the Louis XV period, the slightly later kingwood and marquetry armoire of about 1770 and the marble-top commode or chest of drawers, of similar date. These items may have been part of Lady Braybrooke's inheritance or new purchases in keeping with contemporary English taste. The late sixteenth-century French oak cupboard was bought by Lord and Lady Braybrooke during their visit to Antwerp in 1829 and the green tortoiseshell bracket clock belonged to Sir John. The fine portrait to the left of the armoire is of the Countess of Portsmouth, painted in 1762 by Thomas Hudson. Alongside it is a portrait of Lord Braybrooke's Neville grandfather by Zoffany. Opposite is a portrait of the third lord at the age of twenty-one. Over the years Lady Braybrooke added a group of oval portraits of her children, and prints of relations and friends.

By 1891 Florence, wife of the fifth lord, had added further layers of rich furnishings in keeping with late nineteenth-century taste. The fashion for furniture in the style of the late eighteenth century meant that she could simply bring Sir John's furniture out of storage and have it french-polished and reupholstered. The density of the furnishings is typical of the last quarter of the nineteenth century, the effect increased by table-covers and antimacassars in exotic fabrics and a

collection of antique ceramics. In the twentieth century this became the family sitting room.

15 NEVILLE BEDROOM

Originally the dressing room of the Jacobean State Apartment, this room is one of the few spaces in the house to remain in its original form, with its Jacobean frieze intact on all four walls. In about 1700 the walls were panelled with curved relief (bolection) moulding, part of which survives.

The third Lord Braybrooke probably inserted the Jacobean oak chimneypiece, which evidently originated in a smaller room.

This room and the dressing room beyond now hold displaced furnishings from the Red Bedroom suite on the ground floor, the second-best guest bedroom suite in the nineteenth century. The bed had originally been supplied to Sir John Griffin Griffin in 1766 by the London upholsterer Paul Saunders. The original mixed silk and wool damask still survives on the inside of the tester (canopy) with its shaped cresting. The lacquer furniture and the gilt mirror have always been in the same room as the bed; the night tables are of comparable date, about 1760.

16 NEVILLE DRESSING ROOM

The elaborate low-relief ceiling dates from Sir John's time, when this room served as his wife's dressing room. The door in the outer east wall, like that in the next room, leads through to water closets, further dressing rooms and a staircase to the ground floor.

A number of the portraits are of friends and colleagues of Sir John. On either side of the portrait of the Countess of Portsmouth are views of Hurstbourne Priors, Hampshire, the home of her second husband.

LEFT *Dutch walnut cupboard in the Neville Dressing Room. It has fine ivory and tortoiseshell inlay and was one of third lord's foreign purchases*

CENTRE *Eighteenth-century Boulle-cased clock by Balthazar of Paris in the Neville Dressing Room*

OPPOSITE *Lady Braybrooke's Sitting Room with its French eighteenth-century furniture. The English furniture was added by her successor, Florence, wife of the fifth lord*

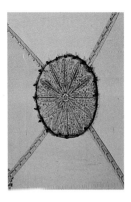

ABOVE *Conventional neoclassical motif embroidered on the inside of the tester (canopy) of the State Bed*

RIGHT *The Howard Sitting Room photographed in the early twentieth century. It is furnished in typical 'country-house' style*

OPPOSITE *The Howard Bedroom. The India blue taffety of the bed-hangings was decorated with embroidery in coloured silk and metallic threads by J Seneschal*

BELOW *Detail of embroidery on the upper valance of the bed*

17 HOWARD DRESSING ROOM

From the third Lord Braybrooke's time on, this and the following rooms formed another suite of rooms comprising a dressing room, bedroom and sitting room. These were guest rooms, and were never as densely furnished with the bric-a-brac of everyday life as the equivalent family rooms. The entire suite was originally carpeted with a fitted Brussels carpet. Sir John built this room to use as his dressing room in 1784, and it continued to fulfil that function as part of the guest suite in the nineteenth century. Like the Howard Bedroom beyond, it now contains an ensemble of furniture displaced from the nineteenth-century State Bedroom suite on the ground floor. The daybed was probably acquired in advance of a visit to Audley End by the Duke of Gloucester and his wife in 1819.

The paintings include a view of Windsor Castle and portraits of the young Countess of Portsmouth, Anne Rainsford and Anne Heydon, ancestors of Sir John Griffin Griffin.

18 HOWARD BEDROOM

In the seventeenth century this was part of the Queen's State Apartment; the surviving Jacobean ceiling is only about a third of its original size. During the nineteenth and early twentieth centuries it served as the bedroom of the guest suite and was furnished with a four-post bedstead with chintz hangings.

It now contains the State Bed, although the bed is, in fact, much too important for the room and has no historical connections with it. The bed, together with the stool, armchairs and the portrait of Queen Charlotte, were all commissioned by Sir John Griffin Griffin for his State Bedroom (now the South Library) in anticipation of a royal visit following his elevation to the peerage in 1784. In the third Lord Braybrooke's time the bed and accompanying furniture were moved to the new suite of guest rooms on the ground floor, where

COUNTRY LIFE

they were used by Mrs Bancroft and her husband during their visit in 1847. Other furnishings and pictures were gradually added to the ensemble, including the gilded gesso table of about 1730.

The State Bed is one of the most important surviving late eighteenth-century beds and was made by the London firm of Chipchase and Lambert in 1786. The curved foot cornice carries a baron's coronet and military trophies while the side cornices display the Howard crest. The lions' masks on the bed unified it with the chimneypiece from the original State Dressing Room (transferred here in the 1820s). The bed-hangings were described by Emilia Clayton, Sir John's sister-in-law, as being 'made up with the greatest taste I ever saw'.

19 HOWARD SITTING ROOM

Since most of its original furnishings are no longer at Audley End the Sitting Room has been recreated, using the evidence of surviving records, in the country-house style of the late nineteenth and early twentieth centuries. The fine mahogany knee-hole 'partner's desk' – with drawers on both sides – is of mid-eighteenth-century date and may originally have come from Sir John's Library. The large oriental black lacquer chest and the smaller seventeenth-century chest on a modern stand may also have belonged to Sir John: like other furniture of his period they became fashionable again in the last decades of the nineteenth century. The small ebonised bookcase with a rosewood veneered top is of the 1820s.

The pictures were probably chosen for this room by the third lord; they are all recorded as hanging here in 1871. They mostly relate to the

ABOVE *The Butler's Pantry, with its original cupboards. The wall colour was traditionally used for service areas because of the cheapness of the pigments*

Neville family, including a 'conversation piece' depicting the second Lord Braybrooke, together with friends and a guide, examining the classical ruins of Rome. The portraits of the Duke of Brunswick and Prince Ferdinand were copied for Sir John, who had served under both princes during the Seven Years' War (1756-63).

20 NORTH STAIRS

Although the stairs are not in their original position and the flights have been narrowed, this is the second staircase to have survived from the Jacobean house. It is plainer than that on the south side, indicating that the rooms it served were less important.

THE SERVICE AREAS

The life enjoyed by the occupants of Audley End over four centuries would not have been possible without the efficient organisation of the service areas. They have remained mostly to the north of the screens passage, as originally devised in the early seventeenth century, although some of their functions have changed as patterns of service have altered. In 1763 a new block, designed by Robert Adam, was built within a walled enclosure adjacent to the house; it housed the brewhouse, dairy and bakery. A new kitchen was also added, linked to the house by a narrow corridor.

As the role of female servants, particularly that of the housekeeper, became more important in the eighteenth century, a housekeeper's room was set up beyond the valet's room alongside the Entrance Hall. There was also a pantry for the storage of food; larders complete with pickling tubs, meat

hook and bread bin; and a scullery with a copper plate rack and swill tub. The kitchen contained a long table in the middle, dressers at each end, chopping blocks, a salt box, smaller deal tables and wood-bottom chairs. The range and oven featured spits and skewers. The kitchen maids' and cook's rooms were over the kitchen.

By 1797 the servants' hall, adjacent to the new kitchen, was furnished with two long deal tables and forms. Beyond was the laundry with a range and iron stove. Further equipment included a mangle, ironing table, wash tubs, drying frame and clothes horse. Most of the servants' accommodation was in the stables but the footman and other senior indoor servants appear to have had bedrooms on the upper levels of the house.

The service areas have been restored as far as possible, but much of the original equipment has gone and the rooms have been converted for other purposes.

21 BUTLER'S PANTRY

The butler was responsible for the upkeep of the family plate, decanters and glasses and for overseeing the service of food and wine. He was even required to ensure surveillance of the silver overnight: in 1797 this room contained a folding bed, with bars at the windows for extra security. In the nineteenth century he was given a separate bedroom in the adjacent room. Plate in day-to-day use would have been locked away in the cupboards, which were lined with baize to protect it from knocks. The furnishings include a pine work table and trays and a large lead-lined sink for the cleaning of plate. The locking chests were used for storing or moving the plate between houses.

On display in the cupboards is a portion of the family plate. In general it is arranged in groups according to its original ownership, as indicated by the crests that were usually added when pieces were commissioned or purchased. This gives a coherent picture of the chronology of the collection and of dining etiquette at different periods.

The first double case contains pieces from the Rainsford family. Anne Rainsford had married James, second Lord Griffin in 1684, and the pieces were part of Sir John's inheritance which subsequently passed into the Neville family. The second case contains the plate given to Elizabeth Griffin during her marriage to Henry Grey, and the third holds items from her second marriage to the Earl of Portsmouth. The fourth and fifth cases display the magnificent plate of Sir John Griffin Griffin, while the sixth contains Neville family silver. The seventh case is densely arranged with similar types of items grouped together, as it might have been put away by the butler, and the eighth contains items bearing the Cornwallis crest, indicating that they were part of Lady Braybrooke's inheritance. The final case contains miscellaneous late nineteenth- and twentieth-century items.

MUSEUM ROOM
(not accessible to the public)

A dressing room in Sir John's time, this was appropriated by the fourth Lord Braybrooke as a private museum to house his considerable collections of objects relating to classical antiquity, geology and natural history. A watercolour of about 1845 *(below)* shows Samian ware lined up on shelves, the remains of a Roman pavement mounted on a plinth, and geological specimens neatly arranged in a display case. The air of scientific enquiry is belied by a highly domestic decorative scheme, complete with wallpaper, curtains and carpet, making the overall impression one of pleasing idiosyncrasy. The room was preserved by the family until the 1950s when most of the collection was sold to a museum and the interior dismantled for administrative use. It is hoped, however, that in future some elements of the fourth lord's arrangement will be reinstated.

Like his father, the fourth lord was essentially an antiquarian, although his academic pursuits focused on somewhat different subjects. These included not only ornithology but also archaeological work on prehistoric British sites, and he was involved in many excavations carried out in Essex and the surrounding locality

22 SMALL DINING ROOM

Used as a steward's room in the eighteenth century, by the late 1920s this had become an informal dining room for the young family of the seventh Lord Braybrooke. It was smaller, warmer and less formal than the first-floor Dining Room, and was also closer to the kitchen. It currently houses the Dolls' House that belonged to the third lord's children.

LEFT *Interior of the Dolls' House. The curtains and bed-hangings were probably made by the third lord's children from scraps of fabric. They carefully imitate the fashionable taste of about 1830*

BELOW *Watercolour of about 1845 of the Museum Room, with its eclectic collections of antiquities, ethnography and natural history*

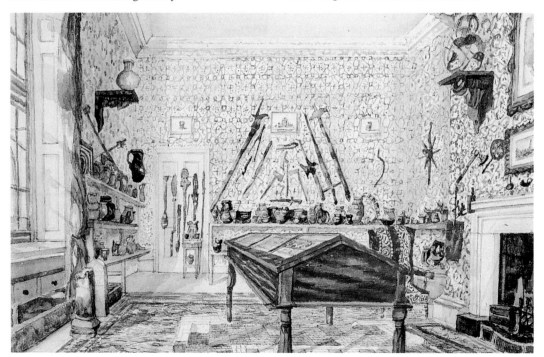

23 LOWER GALLERY

In the eighteenth century an open arcade was erected by Sir John Griffin Griffin beneath the Picture Gallery on the first floor, linking the north and south wings at this level. In 1863 it was enclosed and glazed and the overspill of the fourth lord's natural history cases from the Picture Gallery was housed here.

24 SOUTH STAIRS

This is the richer of the two surviving staircases from the Jacobean period. The third lord stripped it of its eighteenth-century white paint and embellished the newel posts with heraldic beasts. On the stairs hangs one of his most prized possessions: a framed engraving of the Jacobean Audley End. It is one of a series of survey pictures showing the house in its original form, undertaken by Henry Winstanley of Littlebury in about 1676, when Audley End was a royal palace.

The very large painting with the lavish frame is of Billingbear and its environs by Jan Griffier the Younger. This was the ancestral seat of the Nevilles in Berkshire; Windsor Castle can be glimpsed in the background. The house was demolished in 1926.

25 SOUTH CORRIDOR (RED BEDROOM SUITE)

In the eighteenth century the rooms on the north side of this wing were part of the suite of rooms created for Sir John Griffin Griffin by Robert Adam in the 1770s. The corridor was cut through in the

ABOVE The Lower Gallery contains more of the fourth lord's natural history collections

RIGHT One of a series of views of Audley End painted by William Tomkins in the 1780s, following the completion of Lord Howard's alterations

BELOW The bottom of the South Stairs in about 1850. The oak heraldic beasts were added to the newel posts by the third lord

1820s, destroying Sir John's parlours where he had hung his fine collection of Old Master paintings. On the left new servants' rooms were created. At the east end of the wing the former Library was dismantled and replaced by the Red Bedroom suite, containing the Red Bed (now seen in the Neville Bedroom). Adam's grand reception rooms on the south side were converted into a State Bedroom suite, but have since been restored to their late eighteenth-century appearance.

26 18TH-CENTURY TOPOGRAPHICAL PAINTINGS

At the end of the corridor, in the nineteenth-century dressing room, is a collection of views of the house and park, most of which were painted by William Tomkins in the 1780s. The Nevilles took these pictures to Billingbear in the nineteenth century but they returned to Audley End in 1916.

THE ROBERT ADAM ROOMS

In contrast to the work Sir John Griffin Griffin carried out in the Saloon, the Picture Gallery and elsewhere, which demonstrates his desire to retain and emphasise the antiquity of the house, his remodelling of the ground floor of the south wing was intended to create a suite of rooms in the height of neoclassical taste. They were designed by Robert Adam in the mid-1760s and were largely completed and furnished by 1771.

The new suite comprised eight rooms, those on the south forming the 'Great Apartment' while the two on the north provided more intimate accommodation. The design and fitting out of the rooms is recorded in great detail in archives, and their final appearance and function is given in the inventory taken on Sir John's death in 1797.

Unlike the other rooms in the house, which are shown as they have evolved through different

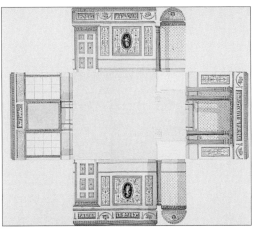

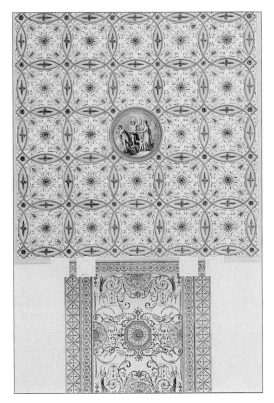

generations, these rooms were reinstated to their eighteenth-century appearance some thirty years ago, leaving no evidence of the nineteenth-century remodelling. Where it survives they are furnished with their original furniture, supplemented by reproductions of the original textiles. The aim is to give an accurate impression of formal late eighteenth-century living, although the exact sequence of rooms cannot be experienced since the principal room, the Library, was demolished in the 1820s. To give a more complete picture of the original furnishings, the 1797 inventory entries for each room have been included in italics below.

27 LITTLE DRAWING ROOM

In all the rooms on the ground floor apart from the Library, Robert Adam was faced with the problem of relatively low ceilings. In the case of the Little Drawing Room this constraint was turned to advantage, resulting in a richly decorated, intimate room ideally suited to its role as a withdrawing room to which the ladies would retire, leaving the gentlemen to continue talking and drinking in the Dining Parlour.

An early unexecuted ceiling design by Robert Adam, inscribed 'Ceiling in the taste of the Paintings of the Ancients', makes clear his aim to create a thoroughly up-to-date neoclassical interior. The decorative painting on the walls, ceiling, doors and shutters is derived from ancient grotesque ornament seen by Adam in Italy, and was executed by Biagio Rebecca in 1773. Rebecca also painted the group of five grisaille panels (monochrome paintings simulating sculpture), which were based on published illustrations of ancient Roman examples.

It is clear from the relationship of the furniture to the architecture of the room, as well as from references in the bills, that Adam was involved in the furniture designs. The suite of furniture was supplied by the London company of Gordon and Taitt in 1771. It is of very high quality water-gilding, as opposed to the cheaper method of oil-gilding. All but one piece has survived (one of two small 'scrole seats'). A comparison of the costs reveals that the most expensive item was not the large scroll-headed couch at £30, but the mirror plate, at £73 10s.

The inventory taken on Sir John's death in 1797 reveals the care taken of such valuable pieces: the furniture had two sets of covers, outer ones of white flannel and inner ones of cotton, which served to protect the precious silk brocade upholstery. The same brocade was used for a wall hanging in the recess, and for festoon curtains which survive, though somewhat cut-down.

LEFT *Set of architectural drawings by Placido Columbani, c.1786, recording the completed decoration in the Little Drawing Room.* TOP *The door, shutter-cases and other details.* CENTRE *Plan and wall elevations.* BOTTOM *The elaborate painting ceiling*

One large Couch, 2 small Do. 2 Bolsters,
2 Pillows, 4 Stools, cover'd with flower'd Sattin,
Cotton & flannel Covers, 2 festoon window curtains
to match, 4 Japan'd Chairs cane seats, a Carpet of
Moores Tapestry, a Piece of Baize for do. A Small
Octagon work table with a Glass top, Carv'd & Gilt
frame, Venetian Blinds, Sattin Hangings for recess,
paper covering to do. on canvas.

28 GREAT DRAWING ROOM

In the eighteenth century this room would have
formed the approach to the even greater richness of
the Little Drawing Room. The lack of height is
more apparent despite Adam's attempts to
manipulate proportions by lowering the dado rail
and reducing the height of the furniture.

The most striking feature of the room is the use of a
three-colour silk tissue for the wall-hangings and
festoon curtains (the existing fabric is a modern copy).
Such rich fabrics enjoyed popularity in the late 1760s.
It was bought from a mercer at a cost of 18s 6d a yard,
almost three times the cost of the silk used in the Dining
Parlour. The fabric itself formed the decoration of
the room and was not concealed by paintings.

Almost the entire suite of furniture, comprising
fourteen pieces of seat furniture and two pier glasses
and tables, survives. It is arranged formally as it
would have been in the eighteenth century; as guests
arrived a footman would have brought forward a
chair for use. These pieces too were protected by
case covers of green-and-white striped linen, while
the marquetry table tops were equipped with
stamped leather covers which would only have been
removed for visitors of the highest status. Some years
after the room was fitted up, green Venetian blinds
were installed to the south-facing windows to
provide further protection to the furnishings.

The group of cane-seated chairs in the bay is a later
introduction. Dating from 1793, they show the trend
away from the grand gilded furniture of the 1760s and
1770s to more informal and easily moveable pieces.

An Axminster Carpet, 8 Elbow
Chairs, 2 Sophas, 4 Window
stools, cover'd with Sattin &
Covers to do. a pair of inlaid Pier
tables, on carv'd & Gilt frames, a
pair of large french plate pier
Glasses in Square gilt frames, an
inlaid pembroke table, 2 fire screens,
8 Japan'd chairs Cane bottoms, a
Plaister Groupe (Venus & Cupid)
by Flaxman, Venetian Blinds,
Sattin Hangings to Room
& paper covering to do. on canvas.

29 VESTIBULE

Entered through the double doors from the
South Stairs, this room would have formed the
route by which eighteenth-century visitors
approached the Great Drawing Room or Dining
Parlour. When looking through the two Drawing
Rooms the extent of the original enfilade or vista
can be appreciated; it would also have taken in
the now-demolished Library.

The Vestibule was always intended as a
circulation room, and was originally sparsely
furnished with a pair of pedestals designed by
Adam to support candelabra. These were moved
to the State Bedroom suite in 1786 and replaced
by a table and set of six chairs.

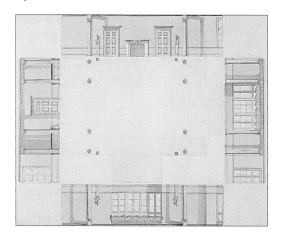

30 DINING PARLOUR

Adam faced even greater difficulties in trying to
create a fashionable interior for the Dining Parlour,
for, in addition to the lowness of the room, the two
Jacobean bays are of different sizes and configu-
rations. To overcome this problem he omitted all
ceiling decoration, and created symmetrical inner
areas defined by the two screens of columns.

The size of the Jacobean windows meant that
shutters could not easily be fitted, so curtains were
provided although this was generally avoided in
dining rooms to prevent smells
from lingering in the fabric.

The curtains also served to
disguise the differences in the two
bays. Originally of lustring (a
glossy silk) matching the pea-
green paintwork, these were
replaced in 1786 by curtains of
green taberay (a silk and linen
fabric), replicas of which hang
here today. By this time fabric
blinds had also been fitted.

The room contains several

OPPOSITE *The Little*
Drawing Room,
decorated with 'grotesque'
ornament painted by
Biagio Rebecca in 1773,
to designs by Robert
Adam. Other ornamen-
tation is derived from
Adam's study of ancient
architecture in Italy

LEFT *Plan and elevations*
of the Dining Parlour,
c.1786, by Placido
Columbani, showing
the original pea-green
colour scheme

BELOW *One of four*
'Window stools' covered
with silk damask which
were provided for the
Great Drawing Room
by the London firm of
Gordon and Taitt

LEFT *One of five chimneyboards painted by Biago Rebecca for the new apartments. It depicts the Borghese vase, a famous antique urn found in Italy. Chimney boards were used to cover the grates when they were not in use during the summer months*

OPPOSITE *The Great Drawing Room, containing its original furniture and hung with three-colour silk damask on the walls. The moulded plaster ornament of the ceiling is by Joseph Rose*

original items of furniture and is arranged as it would have been in the eighteenth century. In contrast to the nineteenth-century Dining Room upstairs, no central table was kept in the room. Instead a variety of tables for different numbers of people were kept in adjacent rooms and corridors and brought in for use. Thus when the room was not being used for dining it could be used as a 'parade room', where costly items such as the carpet could be shown off to their full advantage, and guests might admire the views from the windows.

The carpet is a copy of a rare eighteenth-century turkey-pattern Axminster. The bold pattern and colouring provide a contrast to the dominant colour of the walls and curtains, which are replicas of the 'rich green striped watered taberay' supplied in 1786. As in the Great Drawing Room there were no pictures, though when the Dining Parlour was in use the silver and gilt plate would have made an impressive display.

Twelve Mahy. Chairs, cov'd with leather, a Mahy Octagon dining Table, 2 marble slabs on Mahy. Frames, Four florence Vases on Pedestals, Derbyshire ornaments, & 2 vases, 4 fire screens, a Back do. and Axmr. Turkey Carpet, and Oilcloth, 2 festoon taberay window curtains & balance weights, Blinds, a Grate shovel, tongs, poker and fender, 2 Mahy. Stands for Wine tubs, a painted Chimney Stop by Rebecca.

31 TAPESTRY ROOM

In the eighteenth century this room was a lobby to the Dining Parlour and was used to store extra furniture. Early in the nineteenth century, an important set of tapestries (previously hung in the dressing room next to the State Bedroom) was installed. Woven by Paul Saunders, a Soho tapestry maker and upholsterer, they show figures in a landscape with ruined classical buildings and were supplied in 1767 at the same time as the Red Bed.

To leave the house, retrace your steps through the Great Hall and back into the Entrance Hall.

A HISTORY
OF AUDLEY END

THE MEDIEVAL MONASTERY

The Benedictine priory of Walden was founded in about 1140 by Geoffrey de Manderville, Earl of Essex. In 1190 Richard I raised the priory to the status of an abbey and the original timber-framed buildings were replaced in stone on a new site. The abbey church occupied the site of the present north range of the house while a dormitory, refectory, and abbot's lodging stood where the east, south and west ranges were later built. Thus the abbey buildings defined the basic ground plan of the house in all its later forms.

By the early sixteenth century the abbey had become immensely powerful and wealthy. On 22 March 1538, however, as part of the dissolution of monasteries, it was suppressed and its possessions surrendered to the Crown; five days later they were given to Sir Thomas Audley, Lord Chancellor of England.

SIR THOMAS AUDLEY

The career of Thomas Audley (1488-1544) was one of political achievement and intrigue. He rose from humble origins to hold high office throughout much of the long and turbulent reign of Henry VIII. A lawyer by training, he was judged to be shrewd, of exceptional intelligence, unsubtle, ruthless and, by his own admission, lacking devotion to 'any sects of religion'. This latter was a useful quality in the man charged, as Speaker of Parliament, with overseeing England's break with the Roman Catholic Church.

Audley was appointed Lord Chancellor in 1533 and in the same year conferred legal authority on Henry's divorce from Catherine of Aragon, enabling the king to marry Anne Boleyn. Two years later he passed the death sentence on Sir Thomas More, who had opposed Henry's religious reforms. In 1536 he presided over the trial of Anne Boleyn herself, who was convicted on fraudulent charges of treason and executed in the Tower.

Audley was amply rewarded for his part in the dissolution of the monasteries. He received Walden Abbey and its lands in 1538 and soon set about creating a house within its lofty stone ranges. Much of the church was demolished but the massive nave was retained and three floors inserted into it. The cloister buildings, alleys and courtyard were retained, and a Great Hall was established within the former abbot's lodging, occupying the same position as the Hall in the later Jacobean house. The stables were probably also built in Sir Thomas's time and they may incorporate an earlier monastic building (not a stable). The resulting residence, which Audley described in his will as his 'chiefe and capitol mansion house at Walden', would serve his successors throughout the remainder of the sixteenth century.

ABOVE *Queen Elizabeth I. This copy of the 'Rainbow' portrait, attributed to Marcus Gheeraerts the Younger, hangs in the Saloon. The queen created the barony of Howard de Walden in 1597 to reward Thomas Howard for his naval achievements*

RIGHT *Sir Thomas Audley who, after the dissolution of the monasteries, acquired the lands and abbey buildings which became the site of the future Audley End House*

In 1538 Audley had married his second wife, Elizabeth, sister of the powerful Duke of Suffolk. They had two daughters, only one of whom, Margaret, survived; it was she who inherited Audley End on the death of her mother.

THOMAS HOWARD, FOURTH DUKE OF NORFOLK

Margaret Audley was only four years old when her father died. Her marriage to Thomas Howard, fourth Duke of Norfolk (1536-72), established a Howard link with Audley End which would remain unbroken for almost two centuries. It produced five children, from whom were descended the Earls of Suffolk, Berkshire, Carlisle and Bristol.

Norfolk was an ambitious courtier and close confidant of Elizabeth I. However, he fell from favour dramatically after being implicated in a plot to place Mary Queen of Scots on the English throne, and was executed in 1572. Margaret had

died in 1564 when she was only twenty-four. Following Norfolk's death his brother, the future Earl of Northampton, assumed guardianship of the duke's young children and lived at Audley End. It was probably Northampton who received Queen Elizabeth when she visited the house in 1578.

THOMAS HOWARD, FIRST EARL OF SUFFOLK

Thomas Howard (1561-1626) was the oldest son of the Duke of Norfolk and Margaret Audley. He probably inherited Audley End in 1582. He had an impressive naval career, and was knighted for his part in bringing about the failure of King Philip of Spain's invasion force, the Armada. He was granted the barony of Howard de Walden in 1597.

Following Elizabeth I's death in 1603 Thomas was among the select company which pledged allegiance to the new king, James I. Acceptance at court was critical to political advancement and within two months Thomas was created Earl of

LEFT *Thomas Howard, fourth Duke of Norfolk. Ironically, investigations into his alleged treason were launched while Queen Elizabeth was staying at Audley End in the summer 1569*

LEFT *Thomas Howard, first Earl of Suffolk, from the sequence of family portraits in the Saloon*

BELOW *Portrait of James I from the Audley End collection. James created Thomas Howard first Earl of Suffolk and bestowed on him the highest government appointment of Lord Treasurer*

Suffolk and Lord Chamberlain of the Household. It was essential that he possess a suitable residence by which to promote his personal power and to accommodate the king and his entourage when they visited. In the year of James's succession, therefore, the earl embarked on the construction of what was to be one of the largest houses in England on the site of his grandfather's house.

Work on the palatial new house began in about 1603 and was largely completed by 1614. It is reputed to have cost £200,000, a vast sum when compared with other 'prodigy' houses (those built with the express intention of impressing and accommodating the visiting monarch). By contrast Hatfield House in Hertfordshire, built in 1607 for another of James's great ministers, Robert Cecil, cost only £12,000.

The palace was built in two stages, the first comprising the four ranges round the inner court. While the internal planning reflected conventions dating back to the Middle Ages, the exterior showed an attention to classical symmetry which was relatively new. The important rooms, with their large windows, faced outwards rather than into the courtyard, following the trend set by great houses of the late sixteenth century. The second phase was the addition of the large outer court. These outer ranges were more highly decorated than those around the inner court.

Just as the scale of the house reflected Thomas's ambitions for royal patronage, so did its planning. This was dictated by the needs of a visiting royal household, with the State Apartments on the first floor of the inner court, the family apartments on the ground floor below, and lodgings for the household and servants on the second floor or in the outer court. The house was entered by way of two porches, the one to the south for the king, the one to the north for the queen. Over the doorways are the contrasting symbols of peace (for the queen) and war (for the king). The Great Kitchen was in the outer court.

These entrances led into the Great Hall. Except on rare occasions only servants would have eaten here, with the steward presiding at the high table on the dais. The earl would normally have eaten in a separate parlour. In the south range was the earl's private suite, with a matching apartment for the countess in the north range. Aristocratic marriages were essentially dynastic alliances; such formal separation would have been usual.

Royal marriages, similarly, were diplomatic alliances, so that the State Apartments were required to be separate and almost equally grand. Each of the State Apartments appears to have consisted of a Great Chamber, in which meals would have been taken on grand occasions; a Lobby, leading to the Withdrawing Chamber; a Bedchamber and a Closet. The rooms that faced into the courtyard probably served as a dressing room and servants' room (with access to the backstairs). On grand occasions when royalty or other high-ranking guests were not present Thomas Howard might have used one of these apartments himself.

The outer court contained not only further lodgings, probably only fully used during royal visits, but also what was virtually a house within a house, centred on the north-west pavilion.

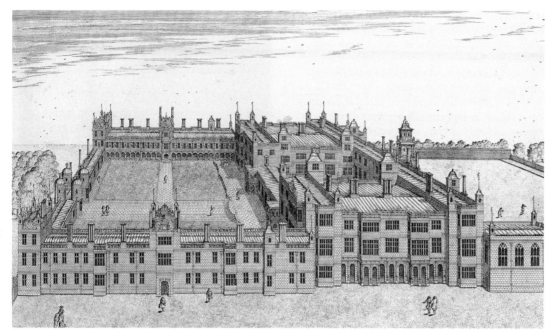

LEFT *Winstanley's engraving of the house from the south. The outer court to the left and the chapel to the right were demolished in the early eighteenth century*

BELOW LEFT *Theophilus Howard, second Earl of Suffolk, who inherited the burden of his father's profligacy*

Accommodation included a Little Hall, Little Kitchen and probably a Little Gallery and Nursery on the first floor.

In 1614, his ambitious new house largely complete, Suffolk was elevated to the position of Lord Treasurer of England. The following year the king visited the nearby university city of Cambridge. Suffolk, as Chancellor of the university, hosted the ensuing festivities at Audley End. James remarked drily that the latter was too great a house for a king, but might suit a Lord Treasurer.

The earl's passion for building and extravagant lifestyle eventually caught up with him: in 1618, amidst whispers of corruption, he was relieved of the office of Lord Treasurer. In November of the following year he was found guilty of 'divers misdemeaners . . . translating of debts . . . extorcion, and bribery', and was committed to the Tower along with his countess, Catherine Knevet. Both were released some nine days later having to pay a fine of £30,000, a sum that was later reduced to £7,000. The earl died in 1626 but his debts outlived him, and subsequent Earls of Suffolk never fully recovered from the disastrous effects of his downfall.

THE SECOND, THIRD AND FOURTH EARLS OF SUFFOLK

The first earl was succeeded by his eldest son, Theophilus (1584-1640). The second earl struggled to maintain his status, but the financial situation was still desperate when his son James, the third Earl of Suffolk (1620-88), inherited Audley

ABOVE *Charles II's Roman Catholic queen, Catherine of Braganza, for whom a separate chapel was created in the former Council Chamber*

RIGHT *Charles II. The king purchased Audley End in 1669 for use as a royal palace, but his interest was short lived*

End in 1640. In the following year the family residence in London (Suffolk House, subsequently Northampton House) was sold and a large quantity of plate pawned, raising about £50,000. Despite this, the deterioration of the estate continued to place great burdens on the family.

When civil war erupted in 1642 James, like many of his East Anglian neighbours, sided with Parliament. He was never fully trusted, however, possibly because of his connection through marriage with the Royalist Earl of Holland, and in 1647 he was accused of anti-Parliamentary activity and imprisoned in the Tower. At the Restoration of Charles II in 1660 the king, perhaps recognising James's underlying Royalist leanings, rewarded him for his 'inconvenience' by the office of the Privy Seal, with its annual income of £2000. This and other court appointments were not enough to secure the house from further decline, and in 1666 it was agreed that the king, attracted to Audley End by its proximity to the racecourse at Newmarket, would purchase the house. A sum of £50,000 was paid, £20,000 of which was to remain on mortgage. Charles took possession in 1668, though the Earl of Suffolk retained much of the adjoining farmland and continued to reside at Audley End as 'Keeper of the Palace'.

CHARLES II AT AUDLEY END

The king's decision to purchase Audley End in 1666 must have been influenced by the fact that it required little modification to turn it into a royal palace. During the autumn of 1668 Charles's queen, Catherine of Braganza, held her court at Audley End. Here she was visited by the king, who spent his time 'divertising himself ... at Newmarket and visiting several forts and towns on the sea-coast'.

In the sixty years since the building of the house, state apartments had become more complex. Access to the monarch, always controlled, had now become extremely selective, and the higher a visitor's rank the further they penetrated into the apartment; thus further rooms were now added. Because certain elements of the original building had never been completed, the suite with the grandest approach was now the northern one and this became the king's apartment, reversing the original intention.

The king quickly lost interest in Audley End, and succeeding monarchs paid it little attention although extensive work was undertaken, much of it under the direction of Sir Christopher Wren, Surveyor of the King's Works. In 1688 the Office of Works carried out an inspection and announced that some £10,000 was required for repairs, although only £500 a year was set aside for their implementation.

In 1701 Wren urged King William III to divest

himself of this unnecessary burden. Accordingly the property was returned to the Howards, though only after Henry, fifth Earl of Suffolk, had agreed to relinquish any claims to the £20,000 which was still outstanding from the original purchase price of £50,000.

AUDLEY END IN DECLINE: THE HOWARDS' RETURN, 1691-1745

The first half of the eighteenth century was one of declining fortunes for succeeding Earls of Suffolk. The fifth earl was seventy-five when Audley End was returned to him, and he died in 1709. His son Henry managed to secure a number of government posts, including First Commissioner of Trade and Plantations (the equivalent of today's President of the Board of Trade) and Lord Lieutenant of Essex. By 1708 he was 'busy to the Utmost of his force in New Moulding Audley End', together with the architect John Vanbrugh (1664-1726), a distant relation.

By now the house was very old fashioned. Changes in the way great households functioned had led to a vast reduction in the numbers of upper members of the household requiring accommodation. The north and south wings of the outer court, containing the servants' lodgings and kitchen, were therefore demolished. The west range was retained, and the small kitchen within its north pavilion now became the principal kitchen of the house. In order to link this isolated building to the main house a subterranean passage was built, part of which survives today. Vanbrugh is thought to have been responsible for other improvements, including the lower arcade of the staircase screen in the Great Hall.

Both title and property then passed to Charles William Howard, the seventh earl. Charles had served as page of honour at the coronation of George I. He succeeded his father to the post of Lord Lieutenant of Essex and seemed destined for high office until his untimely death in 1722 at the age of 29. Charles made further changes to the house in about 1725; the designs are said to have been provided by Nicholas Dubois, a Huguenot refugee. The remnants of the outer court were demolished and a new screen wall, flanked by pavilions (one of which continued to house the kitchen) was constructed. A new chapel was created within the house (remodelled in its present form in the eighteenth century).

Charles had no children, and on his death his younger uncle – also Charles – received the estate, while his elder uncle Edward received the title. The eighth earl was described as having 'great inclinations to versify and some derangement of his intellect'. He mounted an unsuccessful legal challenge to the settlement but the house remained with Charles, who, on his brother's death in 1731, became the ninth Earl of Suffolk.

The ninth earl was described by the eighteenth-century diarist and courtier Lord Hervey as 'wrong-headed, ill-tempered, obstinate, drunken, extravagant [and] brutal'. His wife, however, was a woman of some renown. Henrietta Hobart, daughter of Sir Henry Hobart of Melding Hall, Norfolk and Woman of the Queen's Bedchamber, became the mistress of the Prince of Wales, later George II. She was on poor terms with her husband, not least over the parlous state of their finances, and finally left him in 1717. A long and bitter struggle ensued while Charles sought her return. He was eventually bought off by George II, who paid him £1200 a year via an allowance to Henrietta. In 1728 Charles and Henrietta were legally separated.

Charles died in 1733 and was succeeded by his son Henry, the tenth earl. Remarkably, Henry achieved solvency (a status last enjoyed by the first earl before his downfall in 1619), largely as a result of a dowry of £25,000 arising from his marriage to Sarah Inwen, the daughter of a wealthy brewer. The house benefited from this injection of funds and a number of improvements were undertaken, despite £18,000 being consumed by the earl's inherited debts. In 1736 the open arcade along the south front of the house was enclosed and divided up to form three extra rooms – a dining parlour, drawing room and library.

A NEW ERA: ELIZABETH, COUNTESS OF PORTSMOUTH

Henry was the last Suffolk earl to reside at Audley End; following his death without children in 1745 there ensued a protracted legal wrangle over the rightful beneficiaries of his estate. In 1747 the property was subdivided between a number of recipients, two of whom were grand-daughters of James, third Earl of Suffolk: Elizabeth, Countess of Portsmouth (1691–1762) and her sister, Mrs Anne Whitwell. As part of their share the sisters received valuable agricultural land to the east of the house, while the house itself passed to a different branch of the Howard family. At this stage serious thought was given to demolishing the house altogether or to creating a silk manufactory within its shell.

In 1751, however, Lady Portsmouth secured the future of Audley End by purchasing the house and its immediate parkland. She immediately undertook a range of improvements to secure the building's fabric and improve its standard of accommodation. The London architects Phillips and Shakespear recommended a scheme of demolition and adaptation designed to create a more convenient house plan. The work comprised demolishing the Long Gallery and the pavilions designed by Dubois. A link corridor was built behind the Great

LEFT *Henrietta Howard. The poet Alexander Pope said of her: 'She speaks, behaves, and acts, just as she ought, But never reached one generous thought'*

Hall to provide access to the north and south ranges. The eastern ends of the north and south ranges were reduced to one storey and a new kitchen was created in the north range.

Elizabeth was a forceful character. Having secured the fabric of Audley End, she determined to provide both for the long-term survival of the estate and the continuation of her family name, Griffin. Accordingly she bequeathed the estate to her nephew, John Griffin Whitwell, on condition that he assume the arms and name of Griffin.

Besides Audley End Elizabeth owned another substantial estate, Billingbear in Berkshire. This had been left to her by her first husband, Henry Grey. (Her second husband was John Wallop, Viscount Lymington, created Earl of Portsmouth in 1743.) On Elizabeth's death Billingbear was to pass to Henry's nephew Richard Aldworth, provided he assumed the name and arms of Neville (Henry's own family name). Thus the estates of Audley End and Billingbear, and the Griffin and Neville families, became closely linked.

In 1749 John changed his name by Act of Parliament to Griffin Griffin. Richard Aldworth similarly complied with the terms of his inheritance, so that on the death of Lady Portsmouth in August 1762 both John and Richard inherited their respective estates.

A FORMIDABLE STEWARD: SIR JOHN GRIFFIN GRIFFIN

John Griffin Whitwell (1719–1797) was born at Oundle, Northamptonshire and educated at Winchester School. In 1744 he obtained a commission in the 3rd Regiment of Foot Guards and served against the French army in Flanders until peace was declared in 1748. By 1762 when he inherited Audley End, he had been made a Knight of the Bath, had risen to the rank of lieutenant general and was Member of Parliament for Andover. Injured at the Battle of Campen in Germany, he had effectively retired from active

RIGHT *Elizabeth, Countess of Portsmouth. According to the antiquary William Cole, she was 'as proud as Lucifer; no German princess could exceed her'*

FAR RIGHT *Anne Whitwell, Sir John's mother, was described as kind-hearted and loving, in contrast to her sister Elizabeth*

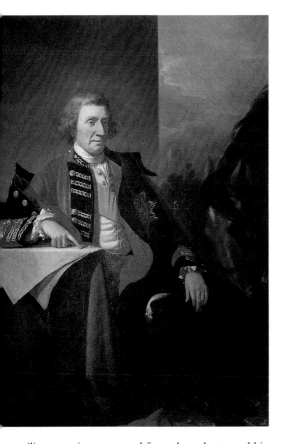

corridor to minimise the risk of fire. Here Sir John's French chef prepared elaborate meals using fresh produce from the extensive kitchen gardens (see page 48). Later a laundry was added (previously clothes and linen had been sent out from the house to washerwomen in the surrounding villages).

The addition of the new kitchen and service block meant that the service rooms on the ground floor of the north range could be rearranged. By 1777 the old kitchen had been converted into a servants' hall while the other rooms were being used for estate and house business, presided over by the steward and butler. In the east bay Sir John built a marble bath. On the first floor above were the private family apartments comprising Sir John's dressing room and bedchamber on the north side and Lady Griffin's dressing room and bedchamber on the south. The entire range was repaired and decorated.

Adam's most notable achievement was the creation of a suite of neoclassical reception rooms for fashionable entertaining on the ground floor of the south range. The suite comprised a Lobby (or 'Anti Room'), Dining Parlour, Great Drawing Room, Little Drawing Room, Vestibule, Library, Water Closet,

ABOVE *Sir John's first wife, Anna Maria Schutz, daughter of Baron Schutz of Sion Hill, Middlesex. They were married in 1749*

TOP LEFT *Sir John Griffin Griffin, painted by Benjamin West. Sir John is wearing his general's uniform and sits in a military tent*

TOP RIGHT *Architectural drawing of about 1755 showing Audley End after the demolition of the Long Gallery*

LEFT *Sir John's second wife, Katherine Clayton of Harleyford, Buckinghamshire was only eighteen when she married Sir John in 1765. He was forty-six*

military service; now aged forty-three, he turned his attention to the renewal of his ancestral home. Sir John was the first owner to inherit Audley End in anything like a sound condition. Nevertheless he spent large sums of money on the replacement of much of the poor-quality stone facing with more durable Ketton limestone from Northamptonshire. But Sir John's ambitions extended beyond keeping the house in good repair. He was interested in the arts and well attuned to the world of metropolitan fashion, and within a few months of his aunt's death he summoned Robert Adam (1728-92) and Lancelot 'Capability' Brown (1716-83) to Audley End. They represented the most advanced taste in architecture and landscape gardening of the day and were asked to collaborate in a thorough replanning of the house and park.

In 1763 the link corridor built for Lady Portsmouth was rebuilt to a wider measure, and a further two storeys were constructed above. This provided communication at all three levels between the north and south ranges. In the same year work began on the service block and kitchen to the north of the house which survive today. Designed or influenced by Adam, the new block housed the brewhouse, dairy and bakery, and was screened from view within a walled enclosure. The kitchen was linked to the house by means of an open

NATIONAL PORTRAIT GALLERY

RIGHT *The fashionable architect Robert Adam, in a portrait attributed to George Willison, 1775*

Sir John's Writing Room and a Supper Parlour.

The Great Hall, the main function of which was now that of grand entrance chamber and staircase, was extensively repaired. An upper screen of plaster, painted to emulate stone, was added to Vanbrugh's stone staircase screen at the southern end of the Hall.

At the same time a new chapel was created in the upper half of the earlier two-storey chapel. It was designed and built by the carpenter John Hobcroft in the Gothick style. This was no doubt thought suitable both for its ecclesiastical connotations and its reference to the Jacobean origins of the house.

By the 1770s Audley End, which had come so near to destruction just a few years before, was re-established as one of the finest houses in the country. The cost of the renewal, spread over some thirty years, amounted to over £100,000 – half the reported cost of the original house. A further £200,000 was spent on running the estate during the same period. To finance this work and the running costs, Sir John was largely dependent on the rents paid by the numerous tenant farmers who worked his estates, which averaged about £3,750 a year. In addition, his residual military duties earned him an average of about £750 a year, while his east coast lighthouse (inherited from Lady Portsmouth) brought in a further £3000 a year through tariffs paid by passing ships. In 1765, following the death of his first wife, Sir John married Katherine Clayton; the dowries from his two marriages brought him £35,000, while a number of inheritances brought further amounts. Though Sir John was not amongst the wealthiest of landowners, his annual income by the time of his death in 1797 had risen to the very substantial sum of about £10,000 a year.

RIGHT *The south-east elevation of Audley End after 1786, following the completion of Sir John's extensive works*

LORD HOWARD DE WALDEN: A NOBLEMAN'S SEAT

Having embarked on the renewal of his family home, Sir John sought to enhance his prestige by petitioning for the reinstatement of the title of Lord Howard de Walden, last held by his great-grandfather, James, third Earl of Suffolk. He was granted the barony by George III in 1784 and in 1788 was further ennobled as first Baron Braybrooke.

Sir John's elevation to the peerage inspired a further series of changes to Audley End, which now had to fulfil the role of nobleman's seat. A further impetus was provided in 1786, when the remote possibility of receiving the king became an apparent certainty. Although this visit never took place because of the king's illness, the summer of 1786 was a period of intense activity at Audley End.

The principal change was the creation of a new State Apartment, sumptuously appointed for the reception of the king, in the south wing. This was approached from the Saloon and reinstated the original processional route from the Great Hall up the Great Staircase. To provide more accommodation Lord Howard raised the single-storey bays at the ends of the north and south ranges by two storeys.

The Saloon was completely redecorated to serve as a grand reception room. Here guests could congregate before dinner, descending the south staircase to enter the Dining Parlour below. By the late eighteenth century dinner would have been served at about four o'clock in the afternoon. When it was over the ladies would withdraw to the Little Drawing Room leaving the gentlemen to talk and drink in the Dining Room. Eventually the groups might reunite either in the Great Drawing Room or the Library for tea or coffee. On less formal occasions guests might have circulated through the ground-floor rooms, dancing, talking or playing cards before taking supper in the Supper Parlour.

Lord Howard died in May 1797 and was interred in the family vaults of St Mary's Church, Saffron Walden. The funeral procession was led by the Revd

Gretton, the chaplain who had officiated daily in Lord Howard's private chapel. Lord Howard had no children and Audley End passed to Richard Aldworth Neville, son of the Countess of Portsmouth's heir at Billingbear. Although they were only third cousins, Lord Howard had ensured that Richard would inherit the barony of Braybrooke. A condition of his inheritance, as stipulated by the Countess of Portsmouth, was that he and his successors assume the name and arms of Griffin.

Richard tactfully hesitated to take up residence at Audley End as this would necessitate the departure of Lord Howard's widow. Lady Howard, however, reassured him that although Audley End had 'afforded her undescribable happiness for thirty-two years, its principal charm is gone', and that 'the best return you can make me is living in this place with comfort to yourself and affectionate recollections of those who have inhabited it with so much delight for such a number of years'. With the arrival of the Nevilles a new chapter in the history of the house began.

RICHARD, SECOND LORD BRAYBROOKE

In 1780 Richard Aldworth Neville, later second Lord Braybrooke (1750-1825), married Catherine Grenville, sister of the first Marquess of Buckingham of Stowe. Like numerous previous owners of Audley End he served as Lord Lieutenant of Essex. He continued Lord Howard's tradition of local good works, endowing a national boys' school in 1815.

With characteristic diplomacy the second lord refrained from making any changes inside the house until after Lady Howard's death in 1809. Thereafter, his modifications were minor and dictated by practical concerns: larger bookcases for the Library and the conversion of the North Parlours into informal sitting rooms.

In 1819 the royal visit for which Lord and Lady Howard had made such careful preparations took place. The Duke of Gloucester and his wife Princess Mary, accompanied by the Duke's sister Princess Sophia, stayed at Audley End for a few days on their way from Cambridge to London. Although the etiquette was much simpler than it would have been in the 1780s, the visit was conducted with great splendour. The house was filled to capacity and thirty-seven people sat down to dinner in the newly adapted Dining Parlour.

Richard and his wife had eight children. One of their sons, Henry, a captain in the 14th Light Dragoons, died in Spain at the Battle of Talavera (1809); he was the first of a succession of Nevilles to lose their lives fighting for their country. In 1819 their

eldest son Richard married Lady Jane Cornwallis, daughter of the second Marquess Cornwallis, and in the following year they moved to Audley End, while the second lord retired to Billingbear.

A ROMANTIC ANTIQUARIAN: THE THIRD LORD BRAYBROOKE

The third Lord Braybrooke (1783-1858) was a Member of Parliament, a scholar and antiquarian, and president of a number of learned societies. In 1823 he edited the first edition of Pepys's Diaries, and in 1836 published his own *History of Audley End* and Saffron Walden. His other great interest was horse-racing and a number of famous racehorses were bred in the Audley End stables, including Sir Joshua, winner of the 1000 Guineas in 1816.

Lord and Lady Braybrooke devoted much of their energy to the house they had inherited, with a particular emphasis on restoring its Jacobean

ABOVE *Richard Neville, later second Lord Braybrooke, pictured with a spaniel in his arms during his Grand Tour visit to Rome, 1773–74. He is accompanied by other young English 'milordi' and the well-known cicerone and guide, Mr Byres*

BELOW LEFT *Richard, third Lord Braybrooke as a young man*

BELOW *The Audley End stablemaster and horses, with the stables in the background, in a mid-nineteenth-century photograph*

ABOVE *'Lemon Leaf 4th', a pedigree cow from the herd established by Charles, fifth Lord Braybrooke*

RIGHT *Mid-Victorian family group outside the State Bedroom. The enclosed arcade gave access directly into the garden*

BELOW *Late nineteenth-century photograph of the house from the south-east, with the parterre or formal flower garden in the foreground*

ambience. Between 1825 and 1835 they carried out a series of alterations that were almost as extensive as those of Lord Howard. There were many reasons for these changes, from essential running repairs and practical provisions such as nurseries for their eight children, to wider considerations of fashion and propriety.

As he discovered more about the magnificence of the Suffolks' palace, the third lord realised the outstanding place Audley End occupied in the history of English architecture. He employed the architect Henry Harrison to help him re-emphasise the house's Jacobean character and purge it of the neoclassical decoration which he detested (though in the event substantial portions of Lord Howard's work were left intact). The internal planning of the house was extensively reorganised, particularly in the south wing, where the principal entertaining rooms were re-established on the first floor – as they had been in the seventeenth century. A new dining room, two libraries and a drawing room were created in the space formerly occupied by Lord Howard's State Bedroom apartments, while, conversely, Adam's apartments on the ground floor were subdivided to provide replacement bedrooms. Adam's Library, the ceiling of which had projected above first-floor level, was subdivided into three rooms and the ceiling destroyed in order to give an even floor level above.

The most important treasures and relics were brought from the former family seat at Billingbear to Audley End. These included portraits, furniture, pictures and a library. Similarly heirlooms inherited by Lady Braybrooke from her father, the second Marquess Cornwallis, found new homes at Audley End. Through the arrangement of these inherited items, together with new purchases and modifications to the house itself, Lord and Lady Braybrooke imposed their distinctive character on

the house. It is their taste that is stamped on Audley End today, many of the rooms arranged and decorated much as they left them.

In 1854 two of Lord Braybrooke's sons died within a week of each other as a result of wounds received during the Crimean War (1854-6). The third lord himself died in 1858 and was succeeded by his eldest son Richard Cornwallis Neville, who survived his father by only three years. The fourth lord, like his father, was a man of learning, particularly in the field of archaeology. He conducted a number of excavations at the nearby Roman fort and villa of Chesterford, excavated long barrows in the vicinity, and discovered Saxon weapons at Little Wilbraham, Cambridgeshire. He was also largely responsible for assembling the impressive natural history collection which can still be seen at Audley End. In an act of family pride, he decided to relinquish the name Griffin and reinstate the Neville name and arms. He was married to Lady Charlotte Toler, but had no male heirs.

In 1861 the fourth lord was succeeded by his brother Charles, whose chief interests were agriculture and cricket. Charles was responsible for laying out the cricket pitch in front of the house in 1842. He also made significant repairs to the house and formed the Lower Gallery in 1863 by glazing in

the open portico on the east front. Charles was succeeded in 1902 by his younger brother, the Hon. Revd Latimer Neville (then aged seventy-five), who was Master of Magdalene College, Cambridge – the college that had been refounded by Sir Thomas Audley in the sixteenth century.

THE TWILIGHT OF AN ERA: THE NEVILLES IN THE TWENTIETH CENTURY

The fate of Audley End in the first half of the twentieth century mirrors that of many aristocratic country houses in England. The collapse of the agricultural economy caused land prices and rents to plummet, forcing many families to dispose of their great houses. Billingbear was demolished in 1926 and from 1904-14 Audley End was rented out. The tenant was, appropriately enough, Lord Howard de Walden (a distant relation), during whose occupancy the house enjoyed an Edwardian swansong in the great age of country house entertaining.

After the lease had expired the seventh Lord Braybrooke returned to his ancestral home with his wife Dorothy and their young family. They carefully preserved the house and its historic contents until the Second World War. On the seventh lord's death in 1941, Audley End was requisitioned for war use by the Ministry of Works, and Lady Braybrooke and her daughter were required to move elsewhere. Both Lady Braybrooke's sons lost their lives in the war: the youngest, the Hon. Robert George Latimer, Ordinary Seaman, was killed in action in 1941 and two years later Richard, the eighth lord, a lieutenant in the 3rd Battalion Grenadier Guards, died in action in Tunisia.

The house and title now passed to the eighth lord's cousin, the Hon. Henry Seymour Neville. By this time, however, Audley End was occupied by the Polish Section of the Special Operations Executive, an organisation so secret that Lord Braybrooke himself was forbidden entry.

THE SPECIAL OPERATIONS EXECUTIVE

For over two years, from May 1942 to August 1944, Audley End served as a secret training station for Polish soldiers, mostly officers, who volunteered to be dropped by parachute into German-occupied Poland to serve in the Polish underground movement. This was part of a scheme conceived by Winston Churchill after the fall of France in mid-1940 to foster resistance throughout German-occupied Europe. Poland was the most distant of the targeted countries and could only be reached by

a flight of some 2000 miles both ways over enemy territory; such operations were possible only in the course of long winter nights.

Candidates were trained in various subjects ranging from guerrilla tactics, sabotage techniques and handling explosives, to radio communications and marksmanship. This was followed by a briefing course in which the candidate was informed of conditions in occupied Poland at the time, and given help in working out an individual cover story to enable him to survive. The work was extremely dangerous: of the 316 agents (including one woman) eventually dropped into Poland, over one-third were killed in action or died, often under torture, in German concentration camps.

One of the rooms in the house was used for making the documents the agents would need when they landed in Poland. The outbuildings were turned into clothing and food stores, and tailors' and shoemakers' workshops.

By the middle of 1944 most operations had been transferred to newly liberated southern Italy which provided shorter and safer routes to Poland. Today the only visible sign of this wartime episode in Audley End's history is the impressive monument near the main drive commemorating the 108 officers and men who paid with their lives for their part in the venture.

AUDLEY END SINCE 1945

During the war the Ministry of Works placed all the furniture in the State rooms and Chapel. In 1945 it was responsible for restoring the house to its pre-war condition.

Before the end of the war the ninth Lord Braybrooke had begun to consider the problem of Audley End's future. He consulted the National Trust's representative, James Lees-Milne, who recorded in his diary a visit to Audley End in June 1944 in the company of Lord and Lady Braybrooke. After some difficulty they gained entry to the house, followed by 'an excellent picnic luncheon' at one of the garden temples. Lees-Milne eventually negotiated the purchase of Audley End for the nation for £30,000 and in 1948 the house accordingly came under the management of the Ministry of Works.

In the 1960s the ministry recreated Adam's Dining Parlour and Great Drawing Room, destroying the bedroom apartments created by the third Lord Braybrooke (a decision which would probably not have been taken two or three decades later). Today English Heritage continues to care for this great house through an evolving programme of research, repair and conservation.

ABOVE *Memorial to the Polish soldiers of the Special Operations Executive who perished during the Second World War. The urn was unveiled in 1983 by the Secretary of State for Defence*

THE GARDENS

OPPOSITE *The landscape of Audley End as it might have appeared in the first Earl of Suffolk's time*

Like the house, the gardens of Audley End have evolved over time to reflect the changing tastes and fortunes of their owners. Besides the story of its own development, the history of Audley End's landscape also tells us something of man's changing relationship with nature, from the Middle Ages to the nineteenth century.

THE FORMATIVE YEARS

The earliest surviving feature in the park is the defensive ditch of an Iron Age encampment, which stands on the ridge beyond the river Cam. During the Roman occupation a settlement was established on the banks of the river. By the late medieval period the landscape was dominated by the stone ranges of Walden Abbey, enclosed by brick walls; today the boundary of the park still follows some of these medieval boundaries. The public roads, which pass close to the present house, had already been established. In the monastic period nature was regarded primarily as a resource, cultivated for use rather than ornament, as evidenced by the fishponds which provided carp for the refectory tables. However, there may have been gardens in the cloister garth at the centre of the abbey, and the grounds would doubtless have included extensive orchards.

Work on the first Earl of Suffolk's gardens probably began in 1614, when his vast new palace was nearing completion, and continued until his fall from political grace four years later (see page 31). Immediately around the house a series of formal gardens was created, many enclosed by newly built brick walls. These provided shelter for a bowling green and for Mount, Wilderness and Cellar Gardens. Beyond these enclosures the monastic fishponds were remodelled to provide vast formal canals, and the meandering river Cam was dammed to create another broad formal canal. New boundary walls and gateways were built, and in the grounds at the front of the house further bowling greens were added and walled cherry and rose gardens were created. Great formal avenues of limes were planted, through which fallow deer roamed (and were hunted).

The formality of Suffolk's gardens reflected seventeenth-century taste: the strict order imposed on the landscape expressed the order of society, with everything having its rightful place in a fixed hierarchy. Avenues led towards the focal point of

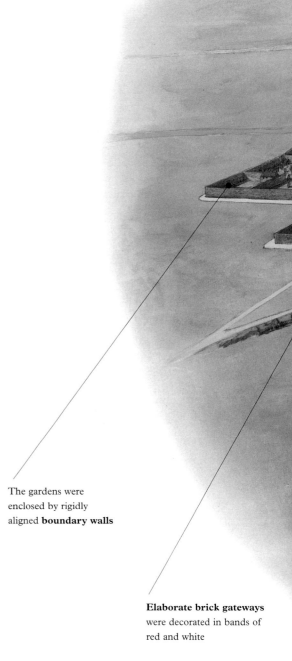

The gardens were enclosed by rigidly aligned **boundary walls**

Elaborate brick gateways were decorated in bands of red and white

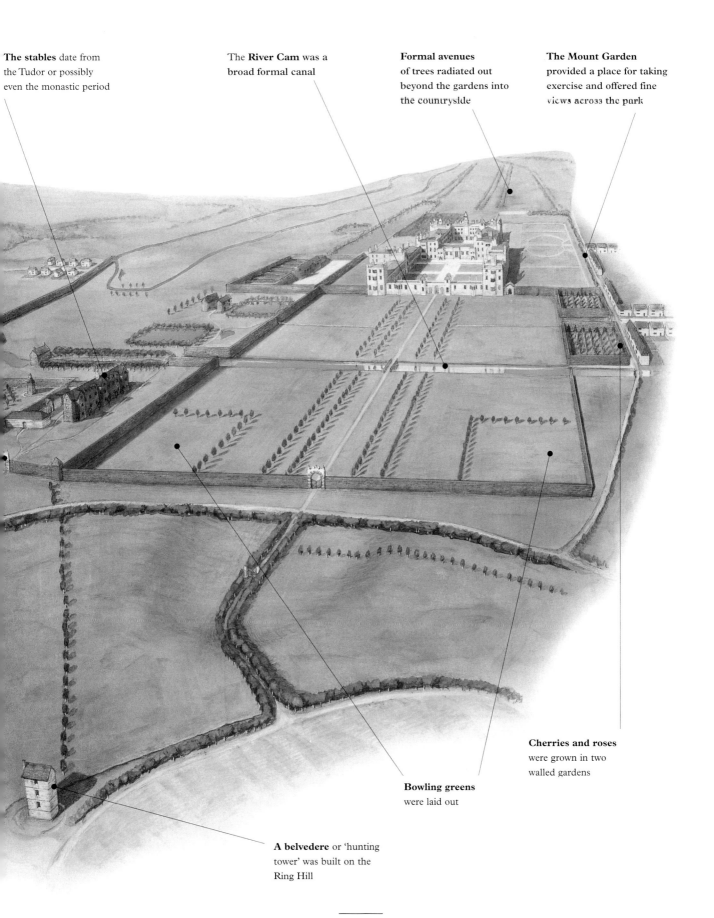

The **stables** date from the Tudor or possibly even the monastic period

The **River Cam** was a broad formal canal

Formal avenues of trees radiated out beyond the gardens into the countryside

The Mount Garden provided a place for taking exercise and offered fine views across the park

Cherries and roses were grown in two walled gardens

Bowling greens were laid out

A belvedere or 'hunting tower' was built on the Ring Hill

the house, whose owner exercised absolute authority over his estate. In the natural hierarchy, man came at the top.

Following Suffolk's downfall the gardens were starved of resources and fell into decline. The diarist John Evelyn noted in 1654 that they 'were not in order'. Things did not improve during the stewardship of King Charles II and by 1701, when the estate was returned to the Suffolks, bridges had collapsed and many of the enclosure walls had fallen.

In 1725 the ninth Earl of Suffolk commissioned a proposal for a vast formal garden. These plans were never fulfilled but a less ambitious scheme was eventually implemented, possibly to a design by the king's gardener, Charles Bridgeman. The main changes were in the old Mount Garden, which was planted with clipped evergreen hedges intersected by broad pathways. The Wilderness and Cellar Gardens were cleared away and supplanted by lawns. The work was probably completed by 1731 when a traveller noted that 'the garden is prettily improved and a very genteel spot, though of no great extent'.

A 'RETURN TO NATURE', 1750-1830

During the late seventeenth and early eighteenth centuries great formal gardens were coming under increasing criticism. The philosophical ideal of man's mastery of nature was being replaced by the idea of man being at one with his environment. The static arrangement of Jacobean gardens was rejected in favour of more fluid planning based on

RIGHT *Robert Adam's 1763 design for the Stone Bridge*

BELOW *The orangery designed for Sir John Griffin Griffin by John Hobcroft, 1773*

Lady Portsmouth's Column, completed in 1774

Glass houses were introduced into the extensive kitchen gardens

The Temple of Victory, completed in 1774

The Elysian Garden, an informal flower garden created in the 1780s, contained various novelties including a cold bath, a tent and a cascade

The Temple of Concord, built in 1790

The river was remodelled in a 'serpentine' form in the 1760s and a new bridge built

The public road was concealed by a **Ha Ha**, which also kept livestock inside the park

Exotic birds were kept in the **Gothick Menagerie** (built in 1774)

ABOVE *The Tea Bridge. A card table was kept in the house specifically for use at the bridge*

RIGHT *Adam's design drawing for Lady Portsmouth's Column*

BELOW *Careful control of the temperature of the glass houses ensured that melons, pineapples, grapes and figs could be produced more or less throughout the year*

MARY EVANS PICTURE LIBRARY

circles rather than straight lines. There was a new emphasis on economy, with calls to turn the wasteful acres of the formal garden to more profitable use by introducing grazing and improved forestry techniques. In this new 'Augustan' age, classical gardens were cited to demonstrate the virtues of combining pleasure with productivity, and it was a short step from here to the introduction of 'classical' buildings into landscaped gardens.

It was in the Countess of Portsmouth's time that the first attempts were made to create an informal landscape at Audley End. The kitchen gardens, formerly near the house, were removed to their present location where they would not offend the eye. In the park, where the formal avenues had already been felled and the timber sold by the impoverished Howards, Lady Portsmouth's gardeners created a more 'natural' appearance with trees planted individually and in clumps.

On his arrival at Audley End Sir John Griffin Griffin immediately set about planning changes to the estate, engaging Lancelot 'Capability' Brown to design and carry out improvements to the park, and commissioning designs for garden buildings from Robert Adam. Brown was the most celebrated garden designer of his day, advising landowners up and down the country on the improvement of their estates. From 1764 he was Master Gardener to George III.

In 1763 Brown began remodelling the park to the front of the house. The last vestiges of the Jacobean gardens were removed while the Cam was remodelled to provide the illusion of a vast natural lake. A **Stone Bridge** designed by Robert Adam was built to replace its Jacobean predecessor. At the same time Brown created an informal garden for Lady Griffin to the sides and rear of the house. It was planted with evergreens and its circular and kidney-shaped flowerbeds were filled with sweet-smelling flowers. A greenhouse (since demolished) and an ornamental dairy (remodelled but still largely intact) added further interest to the scene. Brown was generally on good terms with his clients but his relationship with Sir John turned sour. Brown had been contracted to complete the work by May 1764 but did not finish until 1766; when he submitted his final bill Sir John took exception to a claim for interest. There followed a long and bitter dispute, which resulted in an irrevocable rift between the two and, ultimately, an end to Brown's employment at Audley End.

Following this episode Sir John turned his attention towards modifying Lady

Portsmouth's kitchen garden. A new brick-walled enclosure was built with heated glass houses against its south wall. These were capable of sustaining exotic flowers, vegetables and fruit, including pineapples, melons and grapes, throughout the year. In the early 1770s an orangery (now demolished) was built in the kitchen garden. Here potted orange trees, displayed in the gardens in summer, were stored during the winter months.

In 1768 Sir John appointed Joseph Hicks (of whom little is known) to oversee work in the park. Under Hicks roads were removed, lawns seeded and the slopes within the park gently graded. Thousands of new trees were planted.

THE GARDEN BUILDINGS

Sir John's improvements included the introduction of a number of ornamental garden buildings. These had been largely conceived by Robert Adam in the 1760s as part of Brown's overall vision for Audley End, but construction did not begin until the following decade. They were positioned at the outer perimeters of the park and formed focal points which could be seen from afar. A party making a tour of the estate had the added excitement of being able to see these buildings at close quarters. Here they might stop to take tea, listen to music, play cards or simply enjoy deciphering the inscriptions and motifs which adorned many of the buildings.

The **Temple of Victory** (open for pre-booked guided tours) can be seen from the entrance front of the house. It stands at the edge of the ditch of the Iron Age fort and replaced an earlier hunting tower. Designed by Adam and begun in 1771, it commemorates the Seven Years' War (1756-63), during which Sir John had served as aide to King George II. Inside, an elaborately decorated domed plaster ceiling carries medallions illustrating the glory and consequences of war. The temple was furnished with five curved settees and a marble and mahogany table designed by Adam. There was also a harp, which would have been used to entertain guests while they enjoyed a cold meal of savouries and sweets.

Not far from the Temple of Victory a pavilion containing a **Menagerie** (not open to the public) was built. Here visitors were entertained by the sight of a

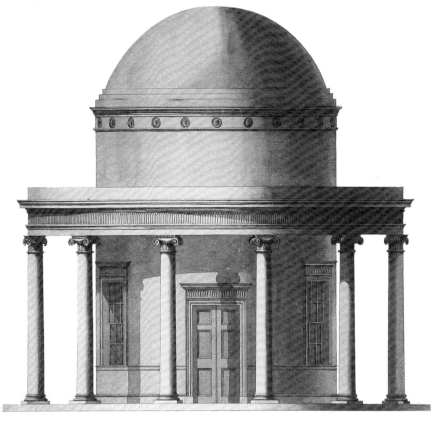

multitude of unusual and exotic birds such as multi-coloured pheasants, eagles, parrots, canaries and goldfinches. The pavilion, in the Gothick style, was completed in 1774. On the ground floor it contained a kitchen, Tea Room and Bird Room, while above were rooms for the keeper and his family. From the comfort of the Tea Room Sir John's visitors could view both the Bird Room and a walled enclosure, where more birds roamed freely.

In 1774 **Lady Portsmouth's Column** was erected in commemoration of Sir John's benefactor. Probably to ensure that the correct site had been chosen, a 'dummy' column of wood plaster and cloth was first mounted where the present structure stands. The permanent structure was erected in great haste: the men were provided with lights to work at night and beer to sustain them. It was adorned with a gilded urn and a carved dedication extolling the virtues of Lady Portsmouth.

In the early 1780s Sir John set about creating a flower garden, known as the **Elysian Garden**, on the banks of the Cam. It was designed initially by

Richard Woods, a relatively prolific landscape designer, but the design was later amended, probably by Placido Columbani, the Milanese architect engaged in decorating the interiors of the house (see page 23). The completed garden was full of delights. Visitors entered by way of a subterranean arch, then progressed through a gloomy evergreen plantation, until eventually they emerged into an open glade.

ABOVE *Adam's design drawing for the Temple of Victory (1771). The twelve Ionic capitals (at the tops of the columns) were carved in Portland Stone at a cost of £49 12s*

ABOVE LEFT *Design drawing for the cascade, attributed to Richard Woods*

LEFT *The Elysian Garden, by William Tomkins, 1788. The garden, a bright open glade, was sheltered by dark evergreens*

ABOVE *Audley end from the west, by Edmund Garvey, 1782. Note the sweeping curve of the river, and Lady Portsmouth's Column to the left*

BELOW RIGHT *The Temple of Concord was designed by Matthew Furze Brettingham and carries plaques extolling the virtues of George III*

Here informally planted beds of sweet-smelling exotics, including roses, magnolias and rhododendrons, were carefully arranged. The garden also contained a Turkish tent, a cold bath (a sunken pool for health-giving bathing), a colonnaded bridge, a cascade and ornamental statuary. Columbani confidently predicted that the garden would 'cherish every plant', since it provided a sheltered situation, had rich soil and an ample supply of water. Sadly, however, it proved to be a frost trap and was largely removed in the 1830s.

Today only the bridge and cascade survive.

By 1786 the remodelling of the park and gardens was largely complete. Miss Emilia Clayton, Lady Howard's half-sister, was sufficiently impressed to write in October 1786: 'The grounds really are delightful and vastly improved'. In 1790 work began on the last of the major monuments to be built during Sir John's lifetime, the **Temple of Concord**, a celebration of George III's return to health after his first attack of 'madness' (now known to have been porphyria, a disorder of the metabolism).

THE RETURN OF FORMALITY

The next owner to make important changes in the park and gardens was the third Lord Braybrooke, who came to live at Audley End in the 1820s. Since Sir John Griffin Griffin's time gardening fashions had changed, and the classical buildings in the park must have seemed alien to early nineteenth-century taste. The classical world and its pagan deities were being replaced by a preference for traditional 'Englishness' and an idealised national past, coupled with a renewed commitment to Christian values. The French Revolution had shaken the English aristocracy profoundly: freedom and 'naturalness' seemed to have gone too far and were succeeded by a renewed desire for order. At the same time there was a growing emphasis on the comfort and happiness of employees, reflected at Audley End in the building of new lodges to house staff.

As part of his scheme of alteration, Lord Braybrooke created a formal flower garden or **parterre** at the rear of the house. Intended to replace the Elysian Garden, this complemented changes that were taking place inside the house, notably the fitting out of a Jacobean-style library on the first floor of the south wing (see page 38). From here the elaborate patterns of the flowerbeds could be seen to best effect.

Advice on the garden was given by the eminent nineteenth-century garden designer William Sawery Gilpin, though the design itself was taken from an eighteenth-century garden pattern book. The original Howard parterres had consisted of nothing more than simple grass beds, but the fashionable revival of Jacobean features favoured a more flamboyant approach.

Preparations for the construction of the new garden were probably under way by 1831, when the estate's expenditure on plants and seeds doubled. The beds were cut in geometric shapes and planted with herbaceous flowers and roses, an unusual and

LEFT *1840s watercolour of the Cambridge Lodge. Completed in 1842, the lodge was of more generous proportions than its eighteenth-century predecessor*

COUNTRY LIFE

ABOVE *The Pond Garden in 1926. The fountain in the fish pond, which has since been replaced, consisted of intertwining fish supporting a shell-like basin*

early example of the parterre revival. In 1865 a further formal garden, the Pond Garden, was constructed. It was inspired by the mid-nineteenth-century romantic taste for rugged landscapes, though the rockwork is entirely artificial. The larger of the ponds was home to a family of otters.

THE KITCHEN GARDENS

During the nineteenth century substantial changes were made in the kitchen gardens. Sir John's greenhouses were demolished and in 1811 an extensive heated vine house was built on the site of Sir John's orangery. A number of other glass houses was added, including an orchard house specifically designed to extend the fruit-growing season. (The orchard house was later demolished but rebuilt in 2001.) The fruit trees were planted in pots on raised beds and the roots pruned annually to limit growth.

By 1884 work in the kitchen gardens was being supervised by the head gardener, Mr Vert. In that year apricots, peaches, nectarines and plums were being grown against the walls. There were about 2,600 strawberry plants and several types of

RIGHT *Flower display in the showhouse, the central section of the restored vine house*

pineapple. Over 250 varieties of chrysanthemum were produced, as well as *Primula sinensis, Salvia patens*, Codiaeums and Dracaenas.

THE PARK IN THE TWENTIETH CENTURY

Few changes were made in the early twentieth century. During the Second World War large areas of the park were ploughed and planted with crops to provide urgently needed food supplies. A number of concrete structures, including a pill box and tank obstacles, were built as part of Britain's east coast defences, known as the General Headquarters Line.

The parterre continued to be maintained until the Second World War when it fell out of use. During the 1980s, following extensive research, English Heritage restored the garden to its mid-nineteenth-century appearance.

Since the Second World War the kitchen garden had been managed as a market garden and had lost much of its nineteenth-century form. In the 1990s work began on the restoration of the vine house and its bothy (worksheds and accommodation for the gardeners), the paths, and the reconstruction of the orchard house. Most recently the main walled enclosure has been replanted, using nineteenth- and early twentieth-century varieties wherever possible.

LEFT *The restored kitchen garden, containing the vine house and orchard house*

BELOW *The parterre, created for the third Lord Braybrooke in the 1830s and restored in the 1980s*

THE PICTURE
COLLECTION

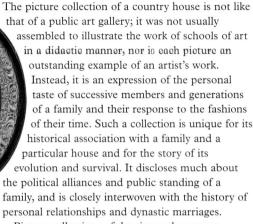

ABOVE *Sir Thomas
Griffin of Dingley by
Nicholas Hilliard, 1599.
This miniature formed
part of the Griffin
family inheritance*

ABOVE RIGHT *Margaret
Audley, Duchess of
Norfolk, by Hans
Eworth, a portrait
acquired by Sir John
Griffin Griffin.
Margaret was the
mother of James, first
Earl of Suffolk, the
builder of Audley End*

RIGHT *The Fourth Earl
of Pembroke, attributed
to William Larkin.
When it was acquired by
Sir John Griffin Griffin
the painting was thought
to portray the notorious
Robert Carr, Earl
of Somerset and second
husband of Frances,
daughter of the first
Earl of Suffolk*

The picture collection of a country house is not like
that of a public art gallery; it was not usually
assembled to illustrate the work of schools of art
in a didactic manner, nor is each picture an
outstanding example of an artist's work.
Instead, it is an expression of the personal
taste of successive members and generations
of a family and their response to the fashions
of their time. Such a collection is unique for its
historical association with a family and a
particular house and for the story of its
evolution and survival. It discloses much about
the political alliances and public standing of a
family, and is closely interwoven with the history of
personal relationships and dynastic marriages.

Picture collections of the sixteenth century
contained mostly family portraits and portraits of
royalty, to the latter of which a family might owe its
position of power and social status. Visiting Audley

End in 1662, William Schellinks saw 'portraits of
the ancestors of the Earls of Suffolk, and of many
kings, of Henry VII, Henry VIII, James, Charles I,
Henry IV of France, Queen Elizabeth and many
other kings and nobles'. Samuel Pepys admired a
portrait of Henry VIII, who had originally granted
Walden Abbey to Thomas Audley. Amidst the
turbulent politics and social changes of the Tudor
period, old established families symbolically
reinforced their claim to eminence by creating
ancestral picture galleries. It was a practice that was
quickly taken up by the new men of power, such as
Thomas Audley. Portraits of successive generations
of family members arrayed in the long galleries of
late sixteenth- and early seventeenth-century
houses testified to a maturing lineage, and provided
an edifying example to their descendants.

The picture collection formed at Audley End by
the first Earls of Suffolk began to be dispersed after
three generations, reflecting the family's declining
fortunes. By 1751, when the Countess of
Portsmouth became the new owner of Audley End,
the house was virtually empty and in a ruinous state.

The collection of paintings assembled at Audley
End thereafter was developed through inheritance
and marriage, as well as by purchase. Its enduring
character was established over three generations by
Sir John Griffin Griffin and later by the third Lord
Braybrooke. It has changed little since, apart from
the addition of new family portraits in the
nineteenth century and the arrival of the last

pictures from Billingbear (the Neville family seat in Berkshire) in 1916. Its multi-layered character displays the pedigrees of the Howard, Griffin, Grey, Neville and Cornwallis families. In addition, Sir John assembled a collection of 'Old Masters' comprising Italian, Dutch and Flemish paintings, mostly of the seventeenth century.

Sir John Griffin Griffin's ancestral collection began with a nucleus of Griffin family portraits from Dingley Hall, Northamptonshire. These were augmented by portraits left to him by his aunt, the Countess of Portsmouth. Her acquisition of Billingbear following the death of her first husband left her with a collection related to the Neville and Grey families, although this remained mostly at Billingbear in the care of her Neville heirs until the early nineteenth century. In the Picture Gallery at Audley End Sir John hung two views of the Earl of Portsmouth's seat, Hurstbourne Priors in Hampshire, which the earl had commissioned from Jan Griffier the Younger. In a comparable act of patronage, Sir John commissioned William Tomkins to paint six views of Audley End and its gardens.

Sir John's ambition to revive the ancient fortunes and Howard titles of his family directed his ancestral collecting towards the acquisition of portraits of English monarchs past and present, and of members of the Howard family associated with Audley End. Some pictures were given to him by friends, such as the important portrait of Margaret Audley, Duchess of Norfolk, mother of the first Earl of Suffolk, the builder of Audley End. The portrait was painted by Hans Eworth in 1562.

The making of copies and secondary versions of portraits was an acceptable way of disseminating images amongst friends, relations and political allies, and many images of royalty were copied for courtiers and gentry. In 1786 Sir John bought portraits of King George III and Queen Charlotte to hang, appropriately enough, in his new State Bedroom and adjacent dressing room. The artist was William Hanneman but they were based on Thomas Gainsborough's portraits at Windsor Castle, which had been exhibited at the Royal Academy in 1781.

The real focus of Sir John's ancestral picture collecting was the Saloon. In the 1770s he commissioned Biagio Rebecca to paint a series of Audley, Howard and Griffin family likenesses (all copies or adaptations of earlier portraits), which were fitted into the panelling of the Saloon. A number of Griffin portraits from Dingley were included, their canvases being extended to fit the panelled recesses. The purpose of this cycle was to illustrate Sir John's and his Griffin ancestors' descent – through the Earls of Suffolk – from Thomas Audley. Sir John is portrayed in a formal manner, standing full-length in the ceremonial robes of a Knight of the Order of the Bath.

A further significant strand in Sir John's collecting was the formation of a collection of 'Old Master' paintings. These display the taste of the eighteenth-century connoisseur, comprising Dutch

ABOVE View of the Valkhof at Nijmegen, *1646, by Jan van Goyen. The third Lord Braybrooke visited the scene of the painting in 1829 and commented: 'I have a picture of Schevening by Vlieger still very like'*

FAR RIGHT *Elizabeth, Countess of Portsmouth towards the end of her life, in a portrait by Thomas Hudson*

RIGHT *The Picture Gallery in about 1850. The third Lord Braybrooke hung a set of Cornwallis portraits here; the natural history cases were fitted soon after this watercolour was done*

and Flemish landscapes and maritime pictures, genre scenes, contemporary Italian pictures of landscapes with classical ruins, and seventeenth-century mythological scenes or religious subjects. Sir John hung these in the two North Parlours, the more private rooms in the wing remodelled by Robert Adam. In this context they were treated as 'cabinet' pictures, precious objects inviting private scrutiny.

Whereas Sir John's collecting activities reflect his interest in family genealogy and contemporary connoisseurship, Richard Neville, third Lord Braybrooke, focused on recreating the interiors of the house in a contemporary and romantic vision of the seventeenth century. He inherited not only the picture collection formed by Sir John, but also

BELOW *Billingbear, the Neville family seat in Berkshire, by Jan Griffier the Younger, 1738. One of a pair of pictures, both of which are thought to have hung in the Countess of Portsmouth's London house*

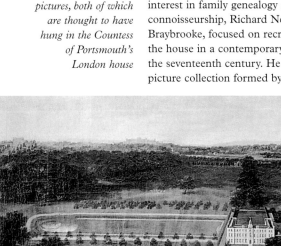

important portraits and other pictures from the Neville family seat of Billingbear, and portraits from the Cornwallis family brought to Audley End by his wife, Jane Cornwallis. Lord Braybrooke revived the idea of a Jacobean picture gallery, where consecutive generations of a family were displayed in affirmation of the continuation of a way of life from one generation to the next: to this end he hung eighteen Cornwallis portraits in the Picture Gallery built by Sir John. Members of his own family were displayed in the new Dining Room, including the most sumptuous portraits brought from Billingbear, alongside those of similar quality featuring Cornwallis family members.

The third lord treated the Great Hall in a similar manner, hanging it with a dense arrangement of family portraits. The three main strands of the collection are represented. Full-length Cornwallis pictures were hung above the panelling, including the second Viscount Townshend, connected to the Cornwallis family by the marriage of his daughter to the fourth baron. Many of Sir John's ancestral portraits are also seen here, pride of place being given to the Duchess of Norfolk. In the late nineteenth century this precious picture was protected by a curtain, drawn across a rod attached to the picture frame. The Neville portraits brought from Billingbear are mostly of sixteenth- and seventeenth-century family members. There are many portraits of monarchs, including James I, Charles II and William and Mary.

The publication of the third lord's *History of Audley End and Saffron Walden* in 1836 and a separate picture catalogue in 1871 provide a valuable record of the location and manner of display of the third lord's picture collection. Lady Braybrooke's dressing room and morning room was hung with a fine portrait of the Countess of Portsmouth by Thomas Hudson, together with portraits of the second and third Lord Braybrookes. A more personal note was struck by a drawing of the third Lady Braybrooke's mother and a series of portraits of Lord and Lady Braybrooke's children.

Lord Braybrooke selected thirty-six of the Old Master pictures acquired by Sir John to hang in his new Drawing Room. The majority of these were Dutch, partly owing to the contemporary taste for Dutch landscape and genre pictures, and partly perhaps because, apart from the Canaletto view of Venice, these represented the best pictures in Sir John's collection. One of the few contemporary family images in the new reception rooms was a portrait commissioned in 1834 by the third Lord Braybrooke of his wife, Jane Cornwallis. The artist was H W Pickersgill who painted a series of portraits of the Cornwallis family.

Almost as important as the pictures themselves was their decorative effect when hung together. In Lord Braybrooke's Drawing Room they were hung against red flock wallpaper, red being thought to provide the most effective background for pictures of this type, with their rich gilt frames. Although picture rails were installed in other areas of the house according to nineteenth-century fashion, Lord Braybrooke followed the practice of his eighteenth-century predecessors by not using picture chains in the Drawing Room. The small gilt labels on pictures throughout the house bear catalogue numbers referring to the 1871 picture catalogue. Audley End never had picture lights as it had no electricity, even during the final years of the family's occupation. The portraits of George II and Charles Cornwallis above the sideboards at either end of the third lord's Dining Room are fitted with brackets to hold some form of lamp or candle sconce, but this was probably intended to light the plate displayed on one sideboard and assist the serving of food and drink from the other.

Although some paintings have been retained by the family and are not on display, very few have been sold. Six Old Master paintings were sold in 1981, of which one was re-purchased for the house in 1993. This is a fine still life by Pieter Claesz, which now hangs in the Drawing Room. Pictures in the Dining Room, the Great Hall, the Picture Gallery and Lady Braybrooke's Sitting Room are virtually as they were arranged in the nineteenth century.

BELOW Still Life *by Pieter Claesz, another fine Dutch Old Master acquired by Sir John, and recently returned to Audley End*

THE NATURAL HISTORY COLLECTION

Modern-day visitors to Audley End are sometimes bemused by the immense numbers of stuffed birds and other natural history curiosities which crowd the glazed cabinets in the Picture and Lower Galleries of the house. While these tableaux may not be to everyone's taste, the displays – swarms of beady-eyed birds naturalistically mounted in elaborate landscape settings – are certainly impressive and constitute one of the most important ensembles of their kind to survive in any country house. They remind us, moreover, of the consuming passion of the fourth Lord Braybrooke and make a notable contribution to the pronounced mid-Victorian character of the interiors at Audley End.

The natural history collections at Audley End were largely formed by the Hon Richard Neville, born in 1820, the eldest son of the third Lord Braybrooke. As well as being a keen amateur archaeologist young Richard took a precocious interest in natural history and appears to have been encouraged in his hobby by his parents. In 1832 they ordered a cabinet for their son's fossils and when he was 15 he was allowed to install his collection of stuffed birds and animals in a series of glass-fronted cabinets in the Picture Gallery. A watercolour by Lady Emily Townshend shows the display, the cases elegantly mounted on stands with turned legs. Most of Richard's specimens were British birds, shot at Audley End or at neighbouring estates and mounted by professional taxidermists, both local and London firms. Some were gifts from relations and friends. A particularly prized specimen must have been a Greater Bird of Paradise, an exotic curiosity which still bears a label – 'This Bird was presented to King William the Fourth by the King of Oude and was alive in England'. The label goes on to relate how its skin passed into the possession of the king's sister, the Princess Augusta, who gave it to Neville at Frogmore. Other specimens appear to have been originally kept as pets, including a Golden Eagle which 'died in the Audley End Aviary'. The Aviary seems to have been a regular source of specimens for the collection – indeed, it may even have been the origin of the taste for taxidermy at Audley End. As early as 1774 it is recorded that Sir John Griffin Griffin ordered that a Golden Pheasant that had died in the Audley End Menagerie be stuffed and sent up to his house in London.

But it is clear from the scale of his acquisitions and the lengths he went to procure specimens that Richard's collection was more that just a youthful accumulation of natural history oddities. An inventory of the mid-1840s lists no fewer than 99 cases of birds, and five years later these were supplemented by a consignment of 136 exotic natural curiosities, sent on the ship *Unicorn* from Fremantle in Western Australia. The specimens, mainly birds but also mammals and reptiles, were sent as skins, packed flat for transport, and were mounted upon arrival. Further expansion accompanied Richard's succession as fourth Lord Braybrooke in 1858 and it was in this year that he embarked upon an ambitious programme of rearranging and rehousing his collection. The Picture Gallery was lined with huge cases, surmounted by strapwork cresting in the Jacobean taste and fitted with panes of plate glass. These were filled with chiefly British and European birds, remounted in extravagant tableaux simulating various habitats by the taxidermist F Butt of Wigmore Street, London. Victorian taxidermists delighted in devising highly fanciful 'naturalistic' settings, constructed out of peat, papier mâché or plaster of Paris, painted or sprinkled with sand and garnished with dried or artificial foliage, and the cases at Audley End are particularly notable in this respect. Meanwhile, the old cases were refurbished and refitted with plate glass to receive the gaudier plumaged foreign birds mounted by R Leadbeater & Son of Brewer Street, London. It is possible that Leadbeater had supplied the Australian specimens, since in the 1850s the firm maintained a branch in Melbourne, 'engaged in collecting largely in every branch of the singularly interesting natural history of that Colony'. The fourth lord died in 1861 but his exotic cases were eventually installed by his brother Charles, who succeeded him as the fifth Lord Braybrooke, in the Lower Gallery, a ground-floor loggia which he had specially enclosed to receive them.

The fifth lord continued to add to the taxidermy at Audley End, patronising the famous taxidermist John Gould (better known for his lavishly illustrated books on birds) for the purpose, and augmenting the collection with old friends such as 'Paddy', an otter, 'purchased when quite young and tamed by Lord Braybrooke during a fishing expedition in Connemara, August 1867', which 'lived afterwards many years in a pond in the Rose Garden'. It was

LEFT *Case containing specimens of two kinds of Bustard, one of a pair of ambitious naturalistic tableaux which guard the entrance to the Picture Gallery*

the fifth lord who, in 1866, compiled a manuscript catalogue of the collection, identifying each specimen by its common and Latin names, supplying additional information about its habitat and provenance. Despite the presence of a serious catalogue the collection never assumed the character of a private museum and a photograph of the Picture Gallery taken in 1891 shows it informally furnished with chairs and occasional tables – as well as a pair of extraordinary firescreens apparently made from squashed swans (which, perhaps not surprisingly, no longer survive). A similar relaxed informality prevailed in the rather more sparsely furnished Lower Gallery and both were clearly intended as comfortable and instructive places to while away wet country house weekends.

Today, changes in fashion and an increased concern about the natural environment makes the Victorian mania for taxidermy as decoration seem strange and unappealing to many visitors. However, the collections at Audley End were amassed in an age when the pursuit of natural history was considered a wholesome hobby and few felt any squeamishness about pressing birds and beasts into the service of interior decoration or personal adornment. After all, hunting trophies in the form of antlers, horns and wild animal heads had long been displayed in country houses and arrangements of 'dried birds' and other natural history specimens were treasured in collectors' cabinets well before the nineteenth century. In the 1770s and '80s the Duchess of Portland amassed a celebrated collection of 'natural and artificial curiosities' at her country retreat, Bulstrode, and in 1802 the Menagerie at Hawkstone boasted 'stuffed birds so nicely resembling nature you can hardly distinguish them from the living ones'. However, little of this early taxidermy survives owing to imperfect techniques of preservation and it was only the introduction of arsenical or 'metallic' soap by the Frenchman Becoeur in 1802 that enabled taxidermists to preserve specimens indefinitely.

ABOVE *One of the crowded displays devised by R Leadbeater & Son in the Lower Gallery. This case contains no fewer than 59 exotically plumaged Australasian birds – presumably those despatched from Australia to Richard Neville in 1845*

This galvanised the development of 'artistic taxidermy' – an art which exploited the decorative potential of displays of preserved birds and animals as ornaments for the home – and ensured its great popularity in the nineteenth century.

When Audley End first came into public ownership in 1948 the natural history collection was seen as an aspect of the unfashionable Victorian taste that was gradually being eradicated from the house. Lord Braybrooke's birds were banished and put into storage as a 'conservation hazard', but were reinstated when the process of restoring the interiors began in the late 1970s. Over the next decade the collection was conserved, each specimen and the interiors of the cases being carefully cleaned. Although the colours of many of the birds have faded, the introduction of blinds in the Lower Gallery will alleviate further damage. The natural history displays at Audley End are a remarkable survival, and their return and refurbishment is a striking vindication of the enthusiasms of the fourth Lord Braybrooke and of the Victorian taste for ornamental taxidermy.

FURTHER READING

PRIMARY SOURCES

Essex Record Office, Braybrooke archives (D/DBy, accession 5859 and temporary accession 1974)
Public Record Office, Works and Lord Chamberlain's accounts, for house as royal palace, 1668-1701
Sir John Soane's Museum, John Thorpe's Book of Architecture; Adam drawings collection

SECONDARY SOURCES

Addison, W, *Audley End* (1953)
Braybrooke, Richard, Lord, *The History of Audley End and Saffron Walden* (1836)
Cornforth, J, 'Victorian views of Audley End', *Country Life*, 8 July 1976
Drury, P J, ' "No other Palace in the Kingdom will compare with it" ', *Architectural History* 23 (1980), 1-39
Drury, P J, 'Walden Abbey into Audley End' in *Saffron Walden: Excavations and Research* 1972-80 (S R Bassett), CBA Research Report 45 (1982), 94-105
Drury, P J and Gow, I R, *Audley End, Essex*, former English Heritage handbook (1984)
Sutherill, M, 'The Garden Buildings at Audley End', 'Buildings of the Elysian Garden at Audley End', 'John Hobcroft and James Essex at Audley End House', *Georgian Group Journal* VI (1996), 102-119, VII (1997), 94-104 and IX (1999), 17-25 respectively
Tipping, H A, 'Audley End', *Country Life* 59 (1926), 872, 916; 60 (1927), 94, 128
Williams, J D, *Audley End: The Restoration of 1762-97* (1966)